How Successful People...
Keep Their Lives Out of The Toilet

Idaho State | University Press

Published by
Idaho State University
Press
Pocatello, ID
in conjunction with

InHomeVations

1578 Cloister Drive
LaHabra Heights, CA 90631
www.InHomeVations.com
fax: 562-690-3170
email: Sandra@Inhomevations.com

ISBN 1-880759-75-6

Dedicated to our mothers
who taught us to stay out of troubled waters—
Opal Ross Aslett
Dorothy Sorensen Savage

ACKNOWLEDGMENTS

Editor: *Eileen Sorensen Carlston, Ed.D.*

Editorial Assistance: *Lee Roderick, M.S.*

Art: *John Caldwell*

Book Design & Art:
Craig LaGory/LaGory Advertising

Production Manager and Layout:
Nancy Everson

Research: *Danielle Doremus*
Natalee Dawn

We thank our families and friends for their contributions of time and insight.

Contents

MW00512076

Foreword

Life in the Toilet. What a revolting concept. How was it ever conceived to write a book that combined life in the toilet with the elusive concept of success? Elusive we ask?

A bunch of soon-to-be graduates were asked why they were breaking their necks (and spending someone's good money) to go to graduate school. Their response, "That's easy. To help us be successful some day."

"What's success?"

The answers came fast, but were all refuted as being too vague. The harder the young people tried to come up with a basic definition of success, the more befuddled they became. Some began to ask, "Why *are* we here?"

A clean-shaven farm boy finally cried out, "It's reaching the top!" His friends, primed for such an answer blurted their own retort, "Where's the top?"

The ravenous pack toppled his definition and every other explanation of what it means to "make it" in life. For each proffered definition of reaching success came an equally convincing example of someone who had achieved "the top" and yet was unhappy, unloved, unmotivated, dissatisfied, and basically unfulfilled in life. No matter the definition, examples can be found of people who seem to fit the success categories but don't "feel" like they are truly successful.

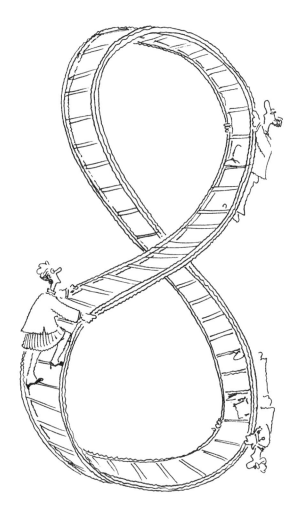

Take the authors for an example. Sandra, an accomplished mother of eight children, has spent her post-collegiate years (Family and Consumer Studies & Communication), changing diapers (spent enough on diapers to have bought herself a new Mercedes), cleaning toilets (seven men in the house), completing scouting projects (six boys, six Eagle Scouts), supporting school activities (at one point she had children in nursery school, elementary, middle, high school and college), and running a one-person taxi service. In the midst of her motherly duties she built two homes (the second, a 5,000 sq. ft. maintenance-free home), served in various leadership positions in her church and the community, traveled and lectured internationally (to six continents), and appeared in a half dozen television segments, all the while fulfilling her role as the wife of a college president—no small task. Having been happily married for more than thirty years, she is also the proud grandmother of six glorious grandchildren.

By most measures, she is "successful" as a mother and is proud that her family bears the brand of her efforts. But she's neither wealthy nor famous—at least not yet. So by other measures, she falls short of being "successful." She may even admit to days when she feels like her life is, "…in the toilet." For example, if you think building a home (or two) can produce a strain on relationships, try writing a book. But the very fact that you are reading this right now proves that she has succeeded as a writer and has been successful in keeping her life (and her book) out of the toilet.

Our second author, Don, is known by several titles, such as, "Latrine King," "Urinal Colonel," and "Don Juan of the John." When Don went to college, he was on his own financially and decided to start a cleaning business to support his noble effort. Inexperienced but bold,

he accepted any offer that paid. Was he successful? Not at first. I laugh every time he tells the story of cleaning wool carpets with hot water and watching the furniture rearrange as the rugs shrank; or using straight ammonia to clean and realizing only too late that the parakeet in a nearby cage fell out of his perch, dead.

Don didn't despair. After graduating from college (English & Physical Education), Don launched a family run cleaning business. With the help of his faithful wife and their six children, this "mom & pop" operation sustained growth and offered a promising future. Don and his partner, Arlo Luke, now own Varsity Contractors, one of the largest professional facility service management companies in North America.

Don's talented enthusiasm is infectious. While managing Varsity Contractors, he has spun off an affiliated business selling cleaning products to the public. He is highly sought after as a presenter on national television and has made appearances on all the current talk shows. He has lectured to innumerable audiences around the globe. Don is a three million-miler member of a major airline. He has been active in community service, served in responsible positions in his church and is a Silver Beaver in the Boy Scouts of America. He takes care of his own ranch in Southern Idaho and spends his winters in the 5,000 square foot, maintenance free home he personally built in Hawaii.

What does he do during the winter in Hawaii? He writes books. I estimate that this book is near his fortieth to be completed. And Don has created his own publishing company—Marsh Creek Press—to assist in moving his works forward. His books have sold more than 3 million copies.

Is Don successful? Like Sandra, in many aspects a resounding, Yes! He is well-known, highly respected, doesn't fret about making it to the next pay check and has been married for more than forty years. But Don also has his days in the toilet. With all else that he has achieved and accumulated, he bristles at the smugness of those who fail to appreciate the nobility of the cleaning industry, and the value of keeping our homes and our world clean.

So, you take a janitor who has made his claim to fame cleaning toilets and a mother who spent her postgraduate apprenticeship in the bathroom cleaning up after the men in her life and what emerges is the genesis of a book on *how to get your life out of the toilet*. It is a natural outcome of a blending of the two authors.

As far as identifying success—Don and Sandra feel it is conduct that creates lasting joy in ourselves and others. Our authors provide direction and inspiration for all of us on how we can more simply keep our lives out of the toilet, which then allows for success.

You will now enjoy an original journey through a delightful array of ideas and applications. I can promise that implementing their ideas and examples will lift anyone's life to a higher level—some of you will even be blown right out of the water. So as you read, pause from time to time for what may be a badly needed flush.

Reed B. Phillips, D.C., Ph.D.
Husband of Sandra

Idaho State University Press

"The Idaho State University Press is pleased to participate in the publication of How Successful People Keep Their Lives Out of the Toilet by Don Aslett and Sandra Phillips. Mr. Aslett was the recipient of ISU's 2000 Distinguished Alumnus Award, the highest honor given by the University. In 1993, the College of Business recognized Mr. Aslett as its Idaho Business Leader of the Year. Since his graduation in 1963, he has been a friend to the University and a role model of ISU students. He regularly speaks to classes, serves on the College of Business Advisory Council, and developed and taught a course for female prison inmates for the College of Technology. His impact at the University is positive and productive."

Richard L. Bowen
President, Idaho State University

CHAPTER 1

Caution: Toilet Territory

WHAT IS LIFE IN THE TOILET?

When we say toilet life, we are not talking about the occasional dips that come with everyday living—the trifling glitches like canker sores, cancelled ski trips, or dead car batteries—we're talking significant unwelcome problems that come and stay until they start making us a toilet dweller. These challenges can be in the form of serious threats to health, demand overload, crushing debt, family friction, trouble with the law, or maybe an ultimate build up of a couple dozen medium-sized things. The toilet doesn't just target the underdog. Top dogs of the community, like ministers, movie stars and long time merchants may live part of their lives in the toilet.

[SANDRA] *My toddlers were about ten months old when they started pulling themselves up to a standing position on things. They held onto the edge of the coffee table, the sofa, and of course, the toilet. It was lower than the furniture and it had that neat little porcelain lip around it, perfect for easy gripping.*

Being a sensible mom, I decided toilets were a bad place to go for infant entertainment. I did my best to keep little Ryan out of the water and issued a bathroom warning to all the older boys—"put the lid down!" And I'd tell the baby, already highly skilled in ignoring maternal counsel, "Don't play in the toilet, it's yucky in there." But the water looked fine to him—cool, made nice splashing sounds—downright inviting.

One day when I thought Ryan was occupied elsewhere, I began to hear the sound of a flushing toilet. The one-year-old dropped several small apples into the bowl and delighted at his new discovery: Each time he pulled the handle to flush the apples, they would swirl, bob around, then pop up to the surface again! He laughed hysterically at the buoyant survivors.

Like these apples, sometimes our lives drop into places we don't want them to be. On occasion we are tossed into the toilet even against our wildest pleadings. But there are other times when we set ourselves up to slide right in. We think it's safe to rim-sit, then lose our balance, and in we go. We swirl around toward the drain with barely enough buoyancy to survive the flush—hardly catch our breath, try to figure out how we ended up in the toilet to begin with—and along comes another flush!

We all face these waterloos. Some self-generated, some imposed by others. Time experts say we spend six years of our life in the bathroom, however we don't want to spend any of it *in* the toilet.

FEW OF US ARE EXACTLY WHERE WE WANT TO BE.

We don't like to admit—not out loud at least—that many of us are dissatisfied. We are driven toward something different, something better, some kind of "more" which we have not yet fully identified.

When we consider the great thinkers, artists and musicians from the past, they are a *consortium* of perfection. This thought can intimidate the average person into non-action. There's just no way to match the noteworthy, grand, and remarkable works of these past masters. The "Greats" truly inspire, but using them as our criterion may be unrealistic.

Their words and works live on as a standard but their lives are gone, while our lives are far from over. *We can still make a difference in our own areas of influence.*

Outstanding qualities in people are worth watching, weighing, and emulating—and they can work for us. There are heroes among our contemporaries with certain traits meant to inspire. But it is useless to sit around and obsess about not being the notable entertainer, businessmen, sports figure, artist, or statesmen. Successful people generate their own dreams and have the confidence and courage to pursue them. They create their individual masterpiece and leave a legacy by developing talents and putting order into their own lives.

We often wonder why we are where we are. At times, the question of why we are one place in our lives and not another, consumes us. To be average or even a little above average, when we compare ourselves with what we *might* be, is toilet torture.

The crowding to see a posting of grades, promotion news, a final team roster, stock report, or anything having to do with a rating confirms our unsettled concern with being at the top.

How many times do we hear people say, referring to others, he or she "has it made"? Probably thousands. But how often do we hear, "I have it made!"? Probably never. We know numerous altogether awesome people, who do not admit to being successful. They may claim success in individual undertakings—even on a major project or two—but are still desperately hunting for something more.

Most of us have a "success inferiority complex." Any victory we achieve seems so meager when compared with others—like the media heroes, ball player millionaires, company heads, and even some of our own neighbors—that we minimize our own successes. We dwell on our struggles and flaws, and downplay our attributes and achievements.

STRUGGLE.

[DON] *Walking down the hall in my new high school right after lunch, some kid came up from behind and kicked me, and then another kid did it, and another. Even one of the school's shy girls took a turn and all of them giggled afterward. What was this? Some kind of an initiation? Finally, after a few more kicks, some merciful little nerd came up and said, "Hey, buddy, why are you wearing that sign?" I felt my back and pulled off a piece of paper with the words, "Please kick me!" written on it. It was the latest high school prank going around.*

The crowding to see anything having to do with a rating or comparison confirms our unsettled concern with being at the top.

Being "kicked" around in life is not something we desire, however it seems like we often wear an unwelcome sign that blurts, "Push me in the toilet." When bad things happen to us, are we simply having a run of bad luck or are we really making bad choices?

In life there are times, places, and situations where we are more careless with our guard than we should be. We get distracted, weary, even lazy and we leave ourselves wide open for a real punch. It's almost like wearing a "Please kick me" sign; or as the saying goes, "You're cruisin' for a bruisin'". None of us intentionally requests to be hit, kicked or pushed, but our vulnerability sometimes allows it.

No matter how well we plan and carry out our lives, we never will be adversity-free. The illusion is unrealistic that someday life will bloom like a flower and overnight all injustice, evil, temptation, reverses, and disappointments will be conquered so we can coast into some hard-earned and well-deserved utopia! The more struggles we survive, the more replacements we seem to find—lots of new, fresh, challenging ones. Despite all the idealistic promises that it is safe to lie down with the lions, we should not leave our guns at home when on the safari of life.

The rich and poor, tall and short, young and old, all take their dips in the toilet because life always involves some adversity. We mourn when we lose a loved one, weep over children gone astray, fall victim to emotional hurts, and anguish over lost opportunities.

The uninvited consequences of ignorance, or other serious setbacks may not be of our own making or are beyond our control. We don't deserve them but they come to all of us from time to time. The list goes on…

- *Medical emergencies*
- *Chronic ailments*
- *Conditions that result from accidents*
- *Genetic disorders*
- *Natural disasters (Mother Nature)*
- *Crime: rape, drunk drivers, terrorists, etc.*

- *Financial reverses; stock market crashes*
- *Untimely death or disease of a loved one*
- *A lemon car*
- *Unwarranted favoritism or harassment*
- *Bad advice from a trusted friend*

"These are the hardest of times"— Winston Churchill.

LANDING IN THE TOILET DOESN'T MEAN STAYING IN THE TOILET.

If we kept a list of the "isn't-fairs" in our life, it could be five volumes long. Like we said, there is always a percentage of happenings that truly aren't our fault. Sometimes we break a bone, contract the disease, or the tornado strikes and we didn't bring any of it on.

[SANDRA] *I became friends with Fausto, a native-born Mexican, who was one of five children from a very poor family. He had a vision problem and was grateful his parents could even afford glasses for him as a child. But by age eleven, his condition had progressed into a nonreversible retina problem that eventually led to blindness.*

"I remember I had to stop attending school in third grade because there were no Braille texts for me and they thought it was a waste of time to teach me anyway."

Four years later Fausto's father met a family from southern California who wanted to give him a chance for education and a dignified future. He was adopted, along with eleven other children like him, into a loving home.

He started school again, at the eighth grade level, and also attended training for the blind at the Braille Institute. He learned English as well as Braille in a new country, with a new family in unfamiliar surroundings.

"This was the hardest time of my life." Fausto said.

After just three years of schooling, the bright young man qualified to attend Cal State University in Fullerton. Amazingly, he walked the mile and a half from his home to the school unassisted. It took him eight years of part-time classes to complete the coursework, but he was able to rise above his predicament and earn his degree. Then he decided to go on to graduate school at Southern California University of Health Sciences. Fausto took a fifteen mile bus ride to the thirty-five acre campus each weekday, where continuous up and down sidewalks and stairs had to be negotiated. He learned his route and made his way with very little assistance, graduating four years later as a chiropractic physician. He is in successful private practice today.

This is the perfect profession for me, as so much of what I do is by touch and feel."

Fausto didn't curl up in the "bowl" and whimper. He moved ahead with resolve instead of remorse, despite his crushing circumstance. Deserved or undeserved, successful people aren't paralyzed by problems.

TO SINK OR SWIM?

The very worst thing we can do when we end up in the toilet is slump the old shoulders and accept our circumstance—the "I'll get flushed if it's meant to be" attitude. Is it adaptive behavior or a self-fulfilling prophecy? It's dangerous when we allow ourselves to feel destined for a toilet life.

There's been a "steady" transition in recent years away from "It's my own responsibility to fix it," to the "I have no control over it," attitude. Years ago we really owned our own troubles. True, we might have whined and tried to blame somebody for a few minutes, but when the cabin burned down, the rattlesnake bit, or the crops froze—we faced it, fought it, and accepted the results pretty well. Nowadays, we label many of our troubles a "disorder" and suddenly, they are not our fault. They are rather the fault of society, the government, God, the company, the partner, the hurricane, the environment, the food, or the advertiser. We have so many bureaucratic agencies to blame things on, we seldom consider our own *free* agency and personal power to handle things!

Even if we are hit with a setback we didn't cause, we may not be able to *change the event or circumstances,* but we can change how we react to it. We have the power to adjust to accidents, crimes, illnesses, and Mother Nature. Adapting is a necessary defense. We can even go on the offense with it, like one young man we know.

A fine photographer, who produced nothing but quality work, lost his eyesight in a freak acid explosion caused by someone else in the lab.

"His career is finished." was the whispered report through all his circle of friends.

"Maybe my photographic career is done for, but watch out."

He revved up his remaining assets and became even more of a success than he had been—a happy, fulfilled writer and lecturer about photography.

This isn't the old make lemonade out of lemons pep talk. It's saying we can expect to taste some toilet water no matter how *good* we are. Our fault? Their fault? Does it really matter? Successful people shed excuses before the dip in the toilet ends up in a flush.

The pleasure of "have it now" blots out the pressure of having to repay someday

There are also vulnerable **times** in our lives when we might make *bad decisions* that lead to *bad consequences.* Be on guard when these circumstances appear.

• *WITH BORROWED MONEY*

The combination of borrowing our way out of a bad situation and the attractive payback time that is usually offered is just enough to push our judgment overboard. We may spend borrowed money foolishly, buying things we can't afford and that we don't really need.

The pleasure of "have it now" blots out the pressure of having to repay someday—and we quickly and silently get in over our heads.

• IN TIMES OF SICKNESS

Doubt, fear, pain, anxiety, disgust, and mistrust crowd in on us and we fall for foolish alternatives, questionable drugs, off-the-wall remedies, crazy trips and all sorts of friend's advice as well as their medications. We even demand excessive legitimate care. "Just give me something to dull the pain, Doc," or "Cut it out so I can get better," or "Give me anything to get me back on my feet."

• AT THE TIME OF DIVORCE

Few people think clearly while in divorce negotiations. Caught up in relief or thoughts of revenge, the need for short-range survival and emotional venting can blot out long-range good judgment. Likely long-term consequences are obscured by the stress of the moment. We like to take sides, not sound advice.

• AT THE TIME OF DEATH

We often make a prompt change to offset the trauma of the event. It's soothes us to move, sell, spend, promise, cut off or add on, instead of waiting until the grief is lessened to make rational, vital decisions.

• DURING "MARTI GRAS" EVENTS

When we celebrate an occasion, it somehow becomes our justification to indulge excessively. We eat, drink, party, pay, bet and love with gusto. We go crowd crazy over contest outcomes, anniversaries or hero holidays that matter very little later.

• WHEN FIRED

The loss of our job (or even just a downgrading of it) often sinks us before reason rules. We say and do things that worsen the situation at hand. We don't cross the bridge to new territory; we burn it to ashes with threats and blame. It's so easy to take the hard stand when the future is temporarily blurred.

• IN TIMES OF LONELINESS

Loneliness builds and is well nourished by more loneliness. In an effort to "unlonely" ourselves, we may yield to temptations and engage in desperate actions before exploring saner options.

• WHEN UNDER THE INFLUENCE

Any drug that muddles our wits and impairs our judgment is a poor source for good decisions. If we are not sane or sober, we're not able to make safe or reliable decisions.

• WHEN IN LOVE

Rapturous feelings can yield sad results. When the heart rules the head, careless passion can punish everyone involved, halt good thinking, and hold progress hostage.

- *IN TIMES OF ANGER*

  Statements made in the heat of anger are usually generalized, exaggerated, and inaccurate. Ugly words or actions may demand malicious obedience, but they don't win respectable followers.

- *IN TIMES OF DEPRESSION*

  Life offers a hazy forecast when you are downcast. If hope slips or is lost, we have little interest in making a decision with the future in mind.

- *WHEN HELPING ADULT CHILDREN*

  We love and feel responsible for our children, but at what age does our obligation to carry their woes stop? We shelter them, sign for them, loan and give over-generously to save them from struggle. Indulgence creates dependence, not self-reliance.

- *WHEN ACTING ON PARTIAL INFORMATION*

  To give in to paranoia and pettiness—to get hung up on the little things (often gossip) and to use this as our intelligence base for decision and action—results in many bad decisions, misunderstandings and inappropriate actions.

- *IN CONTESTS*

  Basic human nature says we don't want to lose. In any competition with others, especially when our own reputation or that of our children is involved, we can easily lose a portion of our good judgment as well as our money.

- *WHEN INVOLVED IN "CAUSE-PHOBIA"*

  Rushing into a new life style, hobby, club, religion, political party, diet, self-help group, exercise program or intellectual clique can catch us up in fanatic fantasies, and cause us to neglect other needful things. Does the new activity enhance balanced lives or pull us away from life?

- *WHEN "HUNGER" STRIKES*

  Desperation for food, as well as position, power, or revenge can blur our sight while we pursue our quest. Uncontrolled appetites of any type ignore the line between wants and needs.

EXCUSES.

"How did I fall in?" we ask ourselves. Some possibilities:

THE DEFEATIST ATTITUDE.

College professors use a couple of big words to explain different views of life. They are determinism and indeterminism. Are we free to choose and be responsible (indeterminism), or is our life planned out for us (determinism or predestination)? For example, we're hard at work changing our flat tire and the jack breaks. We say (determinism) "Well, it just wasn't meant to be that I should change this tire now." More people than we can believe have this fate-destiny "que sera" philosophy of life that our paths are planned, that the outcome is in hands of "the force," and that some of us live cursed lives. Not so—unless we are already in the toilet just waiting for a flush! Deep in their souls, successful people know they are meant to experience joy and that they need to *seek* it from a source higher than themselves—not simply wait for the fate.

I'm just plain cursed when it comes to climbing ladders

IT HASN'T HAPPENED YET SO WHY WORRY?

Perhaps some of you have had a youthful experience with firecrackers similar to this one:

[DON] *We'd light the fuse, toss the cracker down, and sprint off a safe distance to hear the explosion. But there were always a few duds and we called them 'fizzies.' They'd smoke and hiss, and then go quiet as the fuse burned out, and usually nothing more happened. But sometimes a kid would pick one up that was apparently a dud and "Bang!" fingers were injured. I remember the biggest kid warning me, as I reached to pick up a fizzie, "Hey Don, if that fuse is still goin' inside, it'll blow!"*

When the fizzie explodes it's guaranteed to be at the worst possible time, in the worst place, and may take your fingers with it.

Similarly, we can carry around a partially resolved problem that may appear to have been solved, but can surface and explode later when it will do the most damage.

I'm waiting until I hit bottom, then I'll change.

A lot of people are on a Mayday course, getting in deeper and going down fast. They realize they made some dumb mistakes and it's hurting them, but they decide to keep going until they can't go any deeper.

"It'll serve me right. Once I'm bottomed out, I'll fix it, live right, and finally be successful."

[SANDRA] *Jeremy came from a model home, but never quite felt like he measured up to his parents' expectations or his sister's academic and athletic excellence. One day when he felt especially low, he was offered drugs and he began to experiment with them. Before long he used more and more and got seriously dependent.*

Soon Jeremy discovered that by making and selling his own drugs, he could net lots more money and afford a comfortable car and life-style. It wasn't long until the law caught up with him. He then became an embarrassment to his family and qualified for a felony prison record. All of a sudden Jeremy wasn't the only one who had to deal with his problem. His toilet behavior had overflowed into many other people's lives.

Life's bottom is a lot deeper down than we think, and the successful never stay on its downward path.

LAME LAMENTS.

Excuses for our current sorry situations are one of the first things successful people learn to abandon. Don't you just love the old adage, "Never explain, your friends don't need it and your enemies won't believe you anyway!"

Most of us are pretty skilled at making excuses about why we are groveling instead of glorying our lives. Excuse-makers bring what they want *down* to fit what they are. Successful people constantly and quietly work to bring where they are *up* to where they want to be.

> "But I get more sympathy this way. People will help me if I cry long and hard enough about my problems."

Yes, some of us are "professional strugglers" who cultivate problems and seem to love living in the "Loo." This way we attract more attention from mom, the banker, the boss, the minister, and do-gooder agencies than by living free and clear.

But people get really tired of hearing about our trials with our ex-spouse, the landlord, our extra pounds, lack of self-esteem, extra bills, headaches, and other toilet disorders. They tire of constant whining about our inability to make decisions, our weaknesses, our finances, our mate, our busy schedule, our sick parrot, and our sick life. They don't want to hear about our poor health, unemployment, broken fingernails, swearing companions, paper cuts, or the great deals we missed, over and over again. They finally run out of clever sympathy cards. Eventually even charitable people will avoid us—figuring we got about what we deserved.

Continuous toilet testimonials do nothing but give us permanent residence in the bowl. People begin to think we like our swimming spot, and they'll leave us submerged —they won't even be inclined to throw out a life preserver.

One healthy, middle-aged woman we know has about the same number of children and the same financial circumstances as the rest of her neighbors. She also volunteers and works the same number of hours as all her friends but everyone cringes when she engages them in conversation. The intense rehearsal of her busy schedule and personal demands comes spilling out in such gushing laments, no one can take a breath. She is skilled at inflicting her woeful busier-than-all-of-you schedule on every innocent listener.

Why do we avoid people like this? We are plain fed up with the complaints and theatrics they impose on us.

All feeble as well as rational excuses for failure need to be flushed today! Whether we earned all our troubles or not, we have them.

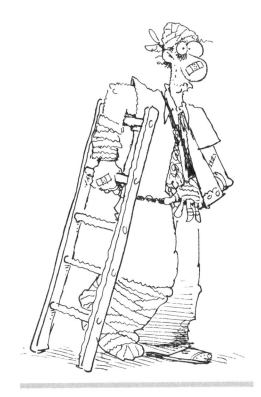

Some of us are "professional strugglers" who cultivate problems and seem to love living in the "Loo."

SHEDDING MORE THAN EXCUSES.

Take 20 people that seem to always struggle in life—the ones who are fluent in the language of constant excuses. You know, the ones that get all the viruses that go around, are first to get laid off the job, have lemon cars, pets in trouble with the neighbors, higher doctor's bills, and are in deeper debt. In short, they seem to be the people that get "all the bad luck." Fifteen out of twenty of these people, regardless of all their excuses, will also be those with more junk, litter, and clutter around them. They will have piles, and stacks of keepables. But for what? They can be kind, religious, smart, and rich people but the majority of their struggle stems from being sunk in excessive stuff; it's almost part of their personality. There are variables or exceptions, but in an overwhelming majority of cases we find that this observation holds true.

Now let's pick twenty other people who seem to have all the luck; the "everything they touch turns to gold" kismet. They seem to get along well, kids mind better, cars run longer, they are respected in the community and things go in their favor more than for anyone else. At least three-fourths of this group will have very little junk, litter, and clutter around. Their places are neat and clean, and they stay that way.

All forty of these folks may be equally good-hearted, well meaning, and deep feeling people; but the fact that junk, litter, and clutter have a negative influence in life's success, is a reality.

CHANGE.

Can you believe how set we all are on changing the world, yet not willing to *change* ourselves? Successful people look inward, give up alibis and change the "something" in their lives they know isn't quite right.

When we say, "it only happens in the movies," we are more right than we realize. Movies leave lots out between the lines. They show a problem quickly solved and its outcome diminished to just hours. We watch the Hollywood handling of a situation and wonder why our own solutions are so slow in resolving or not working at all. Only on the silver screen do men turn from flippant, undependable no-good rogues to responsible, mature husbands after just a chance meeting on a cruise and a kiss. Change is a complex process—like pregnancy—experienced over time and with some serious discomfort. The decision to change can be immediate, but the pathway to reform is usually done with great effort, bit by bit. Bad habits are not easily dropped, and few good habits are easily adopted.

When we decide to make some mighty change we can't overlook the fact that "might" is made up of "mites", tiny little daily disciplines, decisions, sharings, and braveries. Many of these things are hardly visible or detectable, but when added up at the end of the day or a week or especially over a lifetime, they have already transformed into the *"mighty change"*.

> *Change doesn't have to mean a change in location.*

"Let's get out of this place so we can make a fresh start."

The theme for many travel ads, novels, and for that matter lives, is that "away" is the answer to our problems. "Away" seems to be the hidden secret of something better…somewhere. This "greener grass" philosophy has its practitioners always talking about going to somewhere different.

"I just want to get out of this jerkwater town. I want away from this anthill to a bigger, better place where I can shed all the hang-ups and hold-ups in my life for something new, fresh and different." Freedom and prosperity are always "away" in another job, relationship or far-off landscape. Someone else's circumstance always seems superior. Successful people work to enjoy life and bloom where they are planted. The size of the town has nothing to do with the size of people's lives or their ideals.

How many times have we said to ourselves, after thinking about something from the past, and seeing how things worked out, "Boy, if I only knew then, what I know now…." We imagine how we would have changed the world if we had adult wisdom in a young body. Imagine all the good decisions we would have made to live a more perfect and successful life. Well, think of this, we *do* have all that wisdom we wished for! So why not do *now* what we would have done with all our smarts at a smart-aleck age? Change (in ourselves, not our location) can occur at forty, sixty, or eighty as surely as at twenty or thirty, and maybe easier.

The ease of change is largely dependent on two things: cause and commitment. These two virtues enlarge all other abilities, and can only occur after we have shed all excuses.

CAUSE.

We've all seen a certain group of people in action, and have read about their ancestors in history books since the beginning of time. Everyone expresses wonder (even awe) at their persistence, endurance, and inhuman drive. In fact, they seem to work or play even harder when wounded. There are those who just won't quit or get discouraged no matter what the obstacles or odds. They pull strength, motivation and wellness out of the air. They don't fret about eating and seldom whine about the weather, traffic or noise. Even when they are beaten down they are always "up" gritting their teeth instead of bearing their teeth at life's roadblocks.

These people, sometimes referred to as type "A's" (crazy, hyper metabolic, workaholic, extremists)—live for accomplishment. Most of them are and will continue to be successful, and most of us would like to be like them… But they are *so* extraordinary! Or are they?

We learn that these "Icons of Industry" probably have an ordinary mom and dad, and most don't have childhood opportunities or education different from our own. There are even more surprises. Most really don't have any more talent, brains, health, or rich relatives than we do. Noteworthy people are in every detectable way as common as any of us. "Surely, they had a bigger dose of Flintstone Vitamins when young," we cry. Why are they so motivated and successful? Perhaps they've learned some ancient Chinese Soo-goo-cheng-feng secret! But there is actually no mystery or secret here. In fact, we can be their twin for free! Check out any of these successful movers and shakers a little deeper and you'll find out why these people with exactly the same strengths and weaknesses as you and I have are so "outstanding." *Cause* enhances each goal, dream and adventure.

> *"Cause" is where all real courage comes from. When we carry a cause, it quickly begins carrying us! A cause is the only real "magic potion" ever brewed; it is the single most powerful ingredient for success in all areas of our life.*

[DON] *I did a home school convention with my wife, where we spoke, did workshops and sold books in a booth. We had done this type of activity before, hundreds of times, in every part of the country and to every diverse group of people imaginable. After three days, an associate remarked to my wife,*

"Unquestionably, this is the sharpest, most impressive group of women I've ever been around. Every single one of them has something that just radiates control, goodness, and intelligence."

My wife responded, "They have a cause!"

How true! Home-schoolers aren't passive and accepting of "what is" in education. They are out to change things. While most good people have a worthy pursuit, others have a cause. We may work on goals and milestones while theirs is a *mission*.

There is a real difference between a cruise through life and a crusade—just as there's a difference between duty and motive. Good direction is acceptable and necessary, but a sense of destiny is a spark that ignites the soul and sires successful people. Just getting along has some significance in success but getting a cause is compelling passion. It brings stewardship up to a level of ownership and makes life's purpose a religion and not just a club. Working "on things" is not the same as working "for something". The latter—*a cause*—has a deep, worthy value to it. The little key that really catapults moderate men/women into super men/women is the *cause* they stand for and pursue. Cause, not just plain purpose, pushes us to levels we'd never reach otherwise in all five key areas of living: Relationships, Rules, Time, Health and Wealth.

We've seen talent-lacking, losing ball clubs completely sweep the league once they bought into a *cause*.

No matter how good we are with the administrative side of life—our family, the country, our time, our health, and our money, if we can't incorporate an unconquerable drive, things will be on the tasteless side of life. We will not enjoy the success we really want or could attain.

> *Causes cannot be assigned, or inherited; we don't just adopt a membership in a group with a cause. We've got to be fully converted to its mission.*

COMMITMENT.

If there is one word that is beaten to death at motivational seminars, in athletic locker rooms and at church meetings, it is *commitment*—the great solve-it-all word most people try to complicate. No doubt, its magic power has been made too complicated to be useful. We believe the decision to convert a cause into success is possible by doing just one thing, *"Cross the 'I will' line."*

When we're committed, there are no detours, secret passages or slippery side roads—just straight, well thought-out goals that will give great results. Commitment doesn't offer the luxury of convenience, but it lifts and brightens the world of the doer. Commitment bathes him or her in brightness. And soaked in sunshine is a whole lot better than soaked in toilet water.

Regular Life	Committed life
I Wonder... Wish... Want... Wait... Wane... Weep... Whimper	I WILL...

One of the most effective ways to make our commitment sure is to go public, assuming it's comfortable and appropriate to share.

Once we say for all to hear,
- *"I quit smoking this morning."*
- *"I'm going to lose fifty pounds over the next ten months."*
- *"From now on I'm going to wake up at 6 am."*
- *"I will visit you every month, Grandma."*
- *"Watch me cut my credit cards up."*

…we will have 613 energetic, patriotic supporters (actually disciples), to champion our resolve. They'll point out the unwrapped candy in our hand, smell for cigarette smoke, make sure we pay with cash, or ask what time we woke up, all in an effort to help us meet our goals. You just try to eat that Twinkie after you brag (commit) to the whole crew you are off junk food and they will be down your throat faster than you can gulp the grease-stuffed sponge cake.

People love to help each other because service to our fellow humans is one of the big all-time highs. We'll get our best help from others, not by whining or begging for it, but by simply stating our commitment to change or our resolve to produce. With our ensign hoisted, good people will rally to our support.

[DON] *My sister and I worked as partners in the fields picking Idaho potatoes—you know—the great big spuds you see in Sizzler ads. As soon as we arrived at the field, I'd stand at the head of the row and announce to everyone within shouting range that no matter how many spuds they picked, we were going to top them by at least 50 sacks, then we'd work at unbelievable speeds to live up to my promise.*

Right after lunch, laziness crept in and everyone else slowed to a near stop. But my sister and I had to keep going strong. Our honor was at stake. We'd made our announcement and needed to live up to it.

At the end of the season we always got the biggest check and the most praise. We were fulfilled, and credited our success to the honoring of our commitment.

Being middle-of-the-road is one of the common roots at the base of blame for woes in life. We can't learn commitment in a book or from a lecture, or inherit it from bloodlines or borrow it from friends. It's a very personal "within" power—if we don't call it up, it won't serve us.

The regretful news about commitment is that the bigger the commitment bite the bigger the obstacles may be to thwart its accomplishment. It seems the firmer our stand, the plainer target we are for the thrashers of the world to shoot at. (Here come the critics!) It also stands to reason that if we move bigger things, we will be carrying more weight. Commitment doesn't eliminate labor, temptation, or discouragement, or the need for accuracy and judgment, it only guarantees that we'll get the job done. Any pain commitment produces along the way is rewarded tenfold by the pleasure of accomplishing good things.

"Yes! I will."

"I promise."

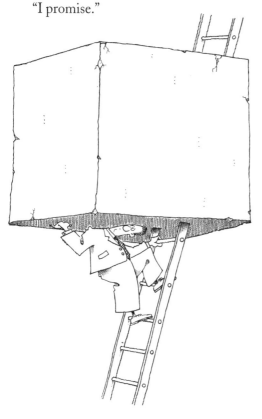

The bigger the commitment bite the bigger the obstacles may be to thwart its accomplishment.

These two phrases are a cure for just about any of our current struggles. Commitment is easy. It's the difference between a thrust in life, and a feeble stab. It's simply saying, "I will" *instead of* "I'll try," or "I'll do my best," or "I'll see what I can do," or "Maybe," or "I'll look into it," or "Gee, I'd sure like to." Anything beyond "I will" is a waste of vital breath.

Commitment is a personal lifesaver that can drag us past our weaknesses. We have noticed when we tell people, "I'll *try*," we seldom produce. But when we say, "I will be there," or "You can count on me," it is usually a 100% guarantee. We are worthless without commitment. As Star War's Master Yoda preached to his Jedi student, "Do or Do not. There is no Try."

Commitment is the easiest way to keep out of the toilet. Once we are committed to something, we'll no longer be bogged down in why's, when's, how's, where's, and what-if's—all of the thrashing that generally has to go on to bring something to pass in life. Commitment draws the shortest line between the beginning and the end of a project. Once you are committed to act, indecision is gone. We've heard it said, "If I really want to do something I'll find a way. If not, I'll make an excuse." With commitment, timing is irrelevant, and accomplishment is a simple matter of arithmetic! Once we decide to accomplish something, it's amazing how swiftly it gets done.

Successful people know commitment forces us to perform instead of just prance around. Commitment might tax us, but it will never cheat us.

"Do or Do not. There is no Try."

Often when we decide to do something, even when we know we've made the right decision and are on the right path, we shiver along the way and say, "Man, I wish I could get out of this." Commitment won't let you. Great accomplishments and character soon result. Everyone benefits. Commitment becomes the cure for cowardice.

DON'T SURRENDER DREAMS.

The bitterest of all times in life is when we feel we must surrender our worthy dreams and direction—those we wanted with all our heart. At such moments, remember that commitment can save them… and us. It can keep us successfully out of the toilet.

In our research, and in our own lives, we've uncovered five simple, universal traits that consistently define successful people. The approach we will take to share these insights is different from other success books because it is slanted to help us realize *subtle areas* where we may fall short, and common areas where we should already be *celebrating the win*. Checklists, charts and real-life stories mark the way as we learn that,

Chapter 2   Successful people recognize and preserve quality **RELATIONSHIPS**
Chapter 3   Successful people keep the **RULES**
Chapter 4   Successful people make the most of **TIME**
Chapter 5   **BODIES** are not burdens to successful people
Chapter 6   Successful people are masters of **MONEY**

"I just don't feel comfortable with him anymore."

"She made me do it."

"This relationship is sucking the life out of me."

"I can't help it—I had an abusive mother."

"This is just the way I am. You'll have to get used to me."

"The boss always did have it in for me."

"I couldn't help falling in love."

"She never listens to a thing I say."

Successful People Recognize and Preserve Quality Relationships

In our day-to-day world composed largely of interactions with others, relationships can be the big numero uno in the whole scheme of things. We might at first think of relationships as being limited to friends, family, and lovers, but in reality we have to include customers, employers, classmates, teammates, our banker, barber, doctor, plumber—even our dog or cat! And perhaps most important of all, our relationship with our Creator.

WELCOME TO THE REAL WORLD.

[SANDRA] *A friend and neighbor of mine, Gary Wallburger, has been in ecclesiastical positions for more than a quarter century now. From his experience in counseling with stable as well as troubled folks, Gary tells me that no one is exempt from eventual problems in one or more of the following areas:*

1. Employment
2. Finances
3. Health, and
4. Relationships

Relationships seem to build up, then fade away as quickly as our bank accounts do. We all know we must ultimately face the death of a loved one, but many of us will also deal with alienation, abandonment, rebuff, unemployment, or divorce at some point. The divorce rate alone outstrips the rates of birth, mortality, inflation, the prime and unemployment combined.

Successful relationships, those full of love and trust—good friendships and joyful companionships—can help insulate us against the pain of other reverses. If we are truly loved and know how to return love, anything out there that needs settling is just a day's work—not a lifetime fight.

Let's consider a few areas of toilet caution in relationships before we explore the can-do builders that successful people rely on to avoid the flush.

DON'T BE CAUGHT UP IN COMPARISONS.

[DON] *My high school basketball team had a four-year losing record—we never even came close to being #1. But all ten of us came out of school winners.*

Is it better up there?

We were educated and ended up in great jobs, married and established families. Second place, or even last place, is irrelevant in some things—life isn't just to keep scores or check ratings or comparisons, or to obtain stuff or status.

Most of us would be happy with our lives and ourselves if we weren't trying to be happier or more satisfied than someone else. Every second, from the inside and the outside, there is an ongoing review of us. We are weighted, rated, ranked, and graded. Our movements are marked and calibrated to assess health, wealth, faith, loyalty, and intelligence. The outcome supposedly determines how *successful* we are. Comparisons!

We live and deal in comparative measurements—like the final fours, top twenties, ideal weight, fluctuating interest rate, size of our family, acceptable salary level and so on. We use our mental energy to statistically analyze every standing conceived by mankind, and do it daily. We literally and figuratively *weigh ourselves* to locate where we are in the overall general standing of societies' acceptables. We make New Year resolutions, and generate charts, sermons, articles and equipment to estimate and validate our standing in every subject from appetites to zodiacs.

Why do we share and display awards, trophies, report cards, trip mementos, diet victories, family pictures, gas mileage results, paycheck stubs, golf scores, promotion letters, the latest fashions, nice stereos, and posh furnishings? *Because they all personify what we believe to be success.* Yet, as we cast one eye to heaven in thanks for these blessings, the other is looking for what we don't yet have.

So we climb up our rungs and constantly check and measure to see where we are and how we are doing. If we are not pleased with our progress, we aren't happy, and if we aren't happy we don't feel successful.

We're so caught up in comparison when it comes to setting our standards and levels of satisfaction that we even envy things we are smart enough to know full well might injure or destroy us. We'll see a magazine with someone famous on the cover who is going through a divorce or rehabilitation, yet we still wish we could be more like him or her. We'll read an article about some billionaire's empire, an entertainer's dream home, a politician's love life, or see a heavily retouched photo of the latest Hollywood babe or hunk, and allow it to set our personal standard of beauty and attainment. Or we'll listen to a relative's glowing account of a high-paying, glamorous job, forgetting that some people exaggerate (even lie), and share only the best angles and greatest stuff for our appraisal. No wonder we slump into insecurity because we "don't measure up." Ironically, many of the folks we eulogize are deep in the toilet trying to pretend otherwise. Media hype trappings don't entice successful people.

Looking the other direction on our personal ladder of success, we see those who don't measure up to our own attainments. We get a certain level of contentment just knowing we aren't nearly as bad as **they** (the low-'rungers'), but still feel twinges of dissatisfaction that we are below the benchmark of other climbers. For most of us, where we rank ourselves on this ladder determines how we feel about our success.

Accepting less than what we perceive to be success is an unhappy personal disaster. We listen daily to people who complain about where they want to be compared to the perceived void of where they are. Falling short of our dreams, expectations, or goals hurts. Period. Are we a worthy father, mother, employee, teacher? Life seems to demand of us some Olympian effort to be "as good as."

With these deep urges to want to do better and feel better, the successful shed some of the treading they've been doing. They run *some* place instead of just *in* place—with the hope to beat haunts and habits that bind them. What we *are becoming* is what counts in life, not where we are in some media line up. If we watch our own feet on the ladder of success, we won't feel a need to analyze other's, above or below us.

THE POWER OF ASSOCIATION.

As kids, we'd often be out of the house, gone for a few hours or even for a day of play, and our parents had no idea which of all of our friends we'd decided to pal around with. Yet that evening back at home, it wouldn't be long until Mother or Dad would say, "You've been

Where is our treading taking us?

paling around with that little Sanders kid today haven't you?" Bingo! Right on. How on earth did they know? We didn't realize this as children, but it was revealed by how we talked, looked, smelled, and by our attitude, the mannerisms and things we brought home from our little rendezvous. The power of our peers to pace and place us is astonishing.

The mother threatening her child was wiser than she knew when she said, "Heather, you hang around that little Philbin girl and you'll become just like her." We all copy our companions in some way, by absorbing and adopting some of their characteristics. *Association is a strong factor in success—or failure.* Some of the most unlikely people on the earth have risen to the best lives imaginable though friendship and association. And some of the most privileged folks have ended up in the toilet through the reverse process.

The "everyone else is doing it" mentality is introduced as far back as the pre-teen years, cultured in high school, and continued with pathetic proficiency into adulthood. When life isn't where successful people want it to be, one of the first things they do is take a good look at whom they're spending their time with. They know if friends are headed toward the sewer, the undertow may well take them along. As a result, we find that people more often end up in the toilet collectively than individually. Positive or negative vibes transfer from one to another without an ounce of planning. People we spend time with we become like, slowly but surely.

Chances for successful life out of the toilet are better if we don't link up with persons who have junk attitudes or aspirations.

[DON] *I worked on a company project in Kentucky for just three days, and spent the next two days fighting an inclination to mimic the locals' drawl in every sentence I formed. "Ah tell ya what…" these things stick. And I'm only in Hawaii a few weeks a year but I find myself using the pigeon slang of the islanders at corporate presentations for weeks after I return. When I'm around gentle, considerate people, their traits too must rub off because others occasionally comment, "Boy, you've been especially kind lately."*

Jesus taught us to love all fellow humans—but He didn't add that we should emulate all of them. Successful people choose and demand wholesome associates who keep them on the path of self-production. Successful people have compassion, treat people well, but are cautious about who they run with in close quarters. Too often we hang around and onto toilet people because of family ties, job, church, or social obligations. In *Clutter's Last Stand*, there is a chapter called, "Junk on the Hoof." The case is made that all junk and clutter in life isn't in drawers or attics, or piled in the garage…people can actually fit this description. They might even be rich, famous, charismatic, and outwardly wonderful, but some can cause problems. They may not mean to cause them but they do. Nursery school to nursing home, there are people lurking around who can clutter our whole existence.

Being with good people at good times and in good places doesn't mean we are some kind of a goody-goody. It means our chances for successful life out of the toilet are a lot better than if we link up with persons who have sewer attitudes or aspirations.

We usually choose who become our friends and associates. Will they be those people dancing on the rim of the toilet or those who are completely out of the bathroom? Chances of getting pushed or pulled in by the rim-sitters are more probable if standing next to them. Successful people don't jeopardize their futures by hanging out with would-be toilet dwellers. That would influence their personal direction—like letting somebody else plan their destiny.

Sometimes we desperately want to start anew. So we change our clothes, schedules, education, location, even vocation, but it doesn't affect our behavior one bit if we don't change our friends (*or the types of friends*) we're drawn to.

We love being around those who inspire us to feel and do better. Those with a pulse and a passion to improve.

SUCCESSFUL PEOPLE DON'T DECK THE HALLS WITH PAST FOLLIES.

It is common to moan to others about our mistakes in life. We share phrases like,

> *"Let me tell you about the time I went to jail."*
> *"I used to be addicted, but look at me now."*
> *"I was the wildest girl in high school."*

Reviving and constantly reconfessing what happened way back when, is really dumb for several reasons. First, few care about the long-past experiences, especially the negative ones—and when we spill our wicked past, it makes others feel uncomfortable. Even if they are interested, what business is it of theirs? And finally, what does it accomplish, really?

It is true that rags to riches, loser to winner, and sickness to health stories are intriguing to hear and tell—everyone loves a success story. And aside from overly detailed surgical or graphic descriptions, these stories are usually welcome and safe to share. But the sensationalistic type of "Sinner to Saved" success story is not always appropriate to spill out for the entire world to hear. Evolving, repenting, and *working toward an increased level of devotion to higher personal values is the ultimate human accomplishment.* And we should be respected for such progress. The problem is too often we dwell on the gory instead of the glory.

If someone rises from the bottom of the toilet bowl, they must be very careful with whom they share the details of their story.

[DON] *A man I worked with told his story to our church congregation. "While I was a Marine, I did what all Marines do, then repented." He visibly shocked the listeners and noticeably reduced his "good example" leadership power. Marines do as many things as our imagination can invent. Turns out the man was not immoral, a carouser, mean or a killer. He later told me he merely picked up a bad language habit then dropped it. But his public "confession" unquestionably weakened his respect in the imaginations of others, especially the youth.*

We see lots of youth leaders, un-wisely dredging up their "wild oats days" for the benefit of their teams, scouts or students, who may end up reasoning, "If our great Coach Chris can survive the wild side, and is tough enough to emerge out of the toilet, so can I."

If someone is an entertainer, business mogul, sports figure or politician, a few busy bodies or hungry reporters might be interested in digging up their old actions. But by and large, most people want to leave another's bygone struggles alone.

Odd as it may seem, most often *we* are the ones who keep opening our old wounds. Other people are quite forgiving and forgetting, but first we must forgive ourselves and let it go.

Our past won't usually come back to haunt us if we follow the steps of saying, "I'm sorry," repaying our debts, returning what was taken and repairing what we have broken, or restoring what was injured. If we keep on reliving our trouble, pretty soon it will be back living with us. This tendency to rehash life's trash will get old with others, too. Letting everyone know where we are and where we're going instead of decking the halls with our past follies is the most powerful message to share.

A TRUE FRIEND.

Friends might disagree with us, but they will stand by us, and look for ways to help us stay on track or get back on track. They are always free and flattered to help us as a counselor or source of information and comfort. True friends are not to be confused with "fair-weather" or "stray cat" friends who might patronize us for some expedient purpose. True friends are friends before, during and after any reverses we might have. Around these friends we don't have to explain or justify. Finding and accepting this type of friend is one of the surest prescriptions for personal success. These friends won't ask us to do anything wrong (or help us do it).

[SANDRA] *Some close friends of mine were raising a fine family of boys. Jim was the oldest, and although he had always been one to push the limits, he wasn't ever purposely on the wrong side of the law. In his late teen years, he got a decent job, and was able to save enough money for his first car.*

Things were going well until Jim told his friends about a gun that his boss kept hidden in a drawer at his work. One of the group begged Jim to 'borrow' it for the night—just take it home for a few hours. Not seeing that any harm could come from the request, wanting to please his friend, and knowing he could have the gun back in place by morning, he produced it for his buddy. The friend used the gun that very night in an armed robbery. The gun was traced back to Jim as the one who stole it from his boss. Jim unknowingly became an accessory to a larger crime as well as indicted for stealing a firearm. He is now facing arraignment.

What seemed a harmless act was blown to catastrophic proportions. Now he has a police record and an uncertain future. A bad personal decision was made worse when a "friend" betrayed him.

Anyone who doesn't want to love or be loved is just a waste of white shirts and shower water, and can never truly be successful. Conversely, no one who has friends to love, and things to do will stay in the toilet. *Relationships are a source of ruin or rescue.* We either cultivate or irritate our connections. How rich our relationships are at home, work, community, or church provide motivation and inspiration, or lead to deprivation.

TOUCHING CAN BE TOUCHY.

The proper time and way to have contact with anyone of any age, in any relationship, can be a tough call. Of course, we need to first recognize that there are cultural differences and expectations. But beyond that, we must be cautious in our efforts to be physically warm and intimate. Successful people do not initiate improper or uncomfortable touching or physical contact. Dancing, for example, can be delightful or degrading, depending on how it's done. Physical contact is a stage of intimacy. Too often extended seconds of sensation sire a sorry situation. In public or private, touching, feeling, lip-kissing, or "too-long" hugs demonstrate excessive familiarity.

Many a toilet trap starts with flirtation, a seemingly innocent interest or admiration. But the little winks, nudges, and trifles that follow are the best seeds available to develop a well-rooted plant. Flirtation is like questionable stock we should have sold off years ago. It starts out strong, then dips, and yields no good returns in the end.

[SANDRA] *A young Arizona mother was able to share her acting and singing talent as the female lead in a community play. She was thrilled with the opportunity. Rehearsals were held nightly for several weeks until everyone learned their parts perfectly.*

Early on, she and one of the male performers who was only a casual acquaintance before the play, developed a close friendship. Within weeks the two eagerly crossed the line into heavy physical affection. Her performance in front of the audience mirrored her newly developed romance off stage. The result was betrayal in both families followed by years of agony and regret.

Successful people know that a little stringing along, a little defying, and a little teasing mixed with deceit and desire breeds breaking the rules.

Conversely, some of us feel entitled to whatever, or whoever, catches our fancy. *Justification implies that we really deserve what we wa*nt. It's very logical and seemingly innocent. As in all seduction, the more results we get, the more intrigued and motivated we are to see how much further we can go.

"I want to play with rattlesnakes but I don't want to get bit."

"I want the honey but I don't want the sting."

"I want to be a boxer but I don't want to get punched."

All are unrealistic desires. Expecting to escape from the reality of outcomes is as illogical as complaining about all the sex movies that play on our home VCR.

Successful people realize that even presidents, who try to set new low-water levels, cannot avoid the eventual flush.

ARE WE "OBSEXED"?

[SANDRA] *While waiting to board a delayed flight one day, my husband and I had a few minutes to browse in the airport news shop. Twelve of the most popular magazines (not to mention any of the sensational rag newspapers) featured cover stories to entice a lonely reader:*
- *After he cheated I married him again*
- *Sex games he'll love*
- *Sex with beautiful women*
- *Sex and the married man: What's really on his mind?*
- *My sizzling affair with my boss*
- *I can't say no to a sexy man*
- *Is my priest the father of my baby?*
- *Sexier Sex tricks he'll love*
- *Secrets to your best orgasm*
- *Very private sex advice*
- *How to satisfy naughty male needs*

We have enough built-in interest in sex without getting additional reminders from movies, music, and the printed news. Successful people know that quality, lasting relationships are not built around the sex act. They also know dabbling in or becoming addicted to pornography or written trash, leads a gratifying relationship toward the sewer.

[DON] *The other day I drove behind a macho man's decked out pick-up. His bumper sticker displayed the "catch and release" slogan, but instead of a fish dangling from the line, there was a silhouette of a nude woman. This playboy (or playgirl) attitude of "catch someone, use and release them," is just plain ugly to the success-minded.*

We've heard the terms "a roll in the hay" or "he's sowing his wild oats." These are more than figures of speech to this Idaho farmer.

Hay was always hot, sticky, and smothering. And once wild oats came up in the field—small, discolored, and ugly—they were almost impossible to remove. They grew and mixed in with regular grains and caused an otherwise quality crop to drop to a low-grade price. Cultivating wild oats or having a roll in the hay exacts a not-so-sweet price to pay, dropping us to a low-grade life.

> *"In bed together" is a union, not necessarily a relationship.*

THE WORDS WE SPEAK.

What we talk about and how we speak says a lot about our standards and values. Our conversation draws people to us, and us to them. It determines the kinds of people we end up with and the situations we end up in.

Further, whom we confide in and what we confide, sets our vulnerability level. Being cautious and wise about sharing our most private, sacred information lessens the chance of unfortunate outcomes.

- *Language has a way of setting the comfort level around us.*
- *Loose with the tongue can mean loose in other ways.*
- *A profane word invites a profane experience.*
- *Trivial talk takes us into trivial circles and idle company.*
- *Sexual conversation ignites sexual contact.*
- *Vengeful and disobedient dialogue develops vengeful listeners.*
- *Crude jokes, gossip, and criticism put us in an un-credible camp where protection is thin. In other words, the more we slide into negative gutter talk habits, the more we are inclined to live that kind of life.*

All TV talk, popular song lyrics, and movie language are not necessarily what we want to model our conversation after. The successful strive to speak in clean, kind language because they know how they express themselves to others does affect the company they attract and keep.

YOU MAKE ME MAD.

Words spoken in anger are often the ones we most regret. We know better, but *lose* it because someone or something "pushed us over the edge."

Genes may play a role here, but the successful do not view biology as destiny. Scientists once believed that people who liked to work hard, who were driven by ambition and tight

Being hostile, critical, and paranoid increases our risk for heart attack!

Those in the high category were 2.5 times more likely than others to have a heart attack or die of heart disease.

[SANDRA] *"Some years ago I caught myself once again yelling at my two small sons. They were fighting over the last clean spoon in the dishwasher that Sunday morning. My frustration turned on those I loved most, and a newly formed habit seemed to be taking over.*

I really didn't want to be a mother who was always screaming at her kids. This particular day my actions felt especially incompatible with the spirit I was trying to bring into our home. My conscience was suddenly deeply pricked and I made a private promise and later, a public commitment to stop my ugly habit. In the weeks and months that followed, I worked hard to keep my promise. Slowly but surely, my yelling stopped. In fact, I feel that patience has become one of my strengths—freeing me to work on other weaknesses. Nowadays, I cringe when moms yell at their kids in the grocery store, or when dads swear at their children when they miss a basket or a goal at the little league game.

deadlines, were the most prone to heart attacks. According to research conducted by one cardiovascular epidemiologist, striving happily and energetically for goals doesn't lead to disease. It's when we snap at people that we are increasing our risk for heart attack!

Another recent study followed nearly 13,000 adults for six years. They were asked whether or not they were hot-headed, felt like hitting someone when angry, or felt annoyed when they were not given recognition for doing good work. Participants were ranked as low, moderate or high in being anger-prone.

When we blow off steam at somebody, they don't soon forget and the backlash will come—probably when we need their goodwill the most.

Control of anger is a choice; it doesn't happen by default, and successful people have learned that. They know that no one else has the ability or power to control our mood and emotions. Flare-ups, bursts of anger, venting, losing it, and letting off steam aren't forced on us by any circumstance. It's all our own doing. It's also the perfect recipe for ending up in the toilet, far away from enduring relationships.

Anger is an emotion we all feel at times, but some have a short fuse that is too easily lit. These folks give in to offensive and damaging outbursts, followed by the same old apologies.

> *Each time we yell at our spouse or hit our kid, we're damaging a relationship that may be the essence of our own reason for living—all because we decided to give into anger.*

When someone says they come "unglued," they cannot better describe the effects of a temper. To become "unglued" is to become unguided and the appropriate way to express feelings is forfeited.

Everyone hates anger—even those who are forever losing their temper hate this habit in others. Temper invites a lower life quality, fewer friends, less of everything except disgusted audiences.

Successful people know that anger burns up energy and that it takes emotion to sustain it. As a driver-training poster in a courthouse once said, "Anger kills"—referring of course to its ability to trigger bad judgment (a fit of anger) in driving—resulting in loss of control, leading to accidents.

In the last decade there's been a 50 percent increase in the rate of aggressive-driving incidents; events in which one driver attempts to kill or injure another driver following a traffic dispute. The American Automobile Association also reports that more than 10,000 injuries result annually from outbursts by motorists who get irked at each other's driving and attack one another with weapons ranging from fists to guns to, in one instance, a crossbow.

Do we make a habit of tailgating, lane hopping, or racing to beat traffic signals? Have we ever aggressively bullied our way through small openings in traffic? Do we find ourselves constantly criticizing and condemning other drivers? These are not traits of the truly successful who know that showing anger injures confidence, judgment, friendship, spirit, trust, health, and opportunity whether we're on the road, in the office, or at home.

We've tried our darndest to discover how a temper might enhance our dealings with our fellow citizens. There seems to be no openings—anywhere. We cannot find a single person who admires or is even remotely impressed with someone who has an immense, well-cultivated temper toward people, traffic, news, lines, weather, or sports contestants. The good news about these misery-making habits is that we have a clear choice. We can totally discard them and flush all their baggage. The toilet is a good place for a bad temper!

CONFRONTATION IN RELATIONSHIPS.

We occasionally feel a real need for confrontation. Something or someone needs to be straightened out or told off big time... those *"we* need to talk" times, when *we* plan to do all the talking. The line here between *having it out* and *having a bit more patience* is a fine one that only the successful have figured out. A showdown at the OK Corral is one thing, but in a relationship that needs to endure, wisdom and patience should usually prevail over western gun slinging. Successful people know when to back off and when to take a stand, but they are experts at avoiding *unnecessary* confrontation.

[DON] *I worked with someone in an office years ago who, no matter how minor the conflict, would call everyone remotely involved into "a meeting" where all facts would be laid out in an attempt to solve the problem. The troubles could be as simple as one person coming late into work, or another talking too long on the phone—things that could have been solved individually. Most of the time things just worsened during the meeting and all left hating each other.*

Left alone, many minor problems disappear on their own. In a showdown, somebody is accused, and there will be a winner and a loser, although even the winner is seldom truly victorious.

Successful people acknowledge but rarely act impetuously on the minor cross-grain bit of grumbling. They avoid wars. We aren't talking cannons and swords here. These skirmishes are the human relations wars fought with pointed words sharpened by rivalry, contention and hostility. These are the picky, piddly vendettas that seem to emerge in all of mankind's daily undertakings, and peck away at relationships. Feuding, or bad blood as some call it, just somehow enters the family, workplace, neighborhoods and even into our recreational pursuits. It may be fueled by competition, jealousy, love or hate—who knows its true source. But when disputes do surface, there are generally different views to the issue. Our first impulse is usually to take a side. This is a bad idea from the beginning, as disputes usually end up in a battle over *who* is right, not *what* is right, and deeper into the toilet we go.

Many people, fired up and trained by a controversy-loving media, delight in dwelling on and dramatizing the "sides" of an issue, creating debates and doubts. Disputes are popular entertainments— people buy books and watch plays and TV programs about "battles" in offices, courtrooms, politics, sports and relationships. But in reality, fights do little but waste time and emotion. They result in loss of friends, business, health, and money. Little is ever gained by hostility. *Successful people stay out of battles.*

"Turn the other cheek" is sound advice, if we are turning to look for something or someone better to have dealings with. We've all seen staggering lawsuits and disputes over tiny, petty disagreements like ten inches worth of property line or five undocumented hours on a paycheck. Often it wouldn't cost much to swallow our pride and settle. Instead people go to battle on what they call *principle* (it's actually *preference*) and end up in prolonged mental agony with tens of thousands of dollars worth of expense.

Successful people don't join in – they fix weighty problems that need to be fixed, and ignore the other petty 95 percent. They don't wage battles with anyone. They don't want their days to be scraps of living leftover after combat.

DEALING WITH DEALS.

Even in the "perfect job" or home life there are often politics to cope with. When merit gives way to manipulation, or favoritism leads to an unfair advantage, relationships are challenged.

Illegal or immoral payoffs don't start with money. They start with granting and allowing exceptions because there can be an advantage *later*. Truly successful people steer clear of such *deals*. They don't seek the front of the line or special favors. Any relationship rooted in political advantage can render us unstable—put us smack in the middle of Obligation City—right next door to Toilet Town. Smart, capable, successful people earn and work their way into jobs

If we sneak in on someone else's ticket, even if we achieve our empire, we must face the fact that our whole foundation was built on someone else's assets.

and opportunities through the front door. It may often take a little longer, but the satisfaction is greater. So is the security. Piggybacking into a position is a coward's way to assure and keep a job. Political favor always has a big price—one that we pay forever. Self-push beats political-pull any day.

> *Playing politics anywhere, at the office, on the ball field, in the home, or in friendships, seldom pays off. Successful people avoid relationship favoritism.*

Most people expect to give a fair day's work for their pay, appreciate their jobs, and respect their co-workers and boss. But there are computer virus-type personalities, who swiftly infect an entire operation negatively. There are also workplace Godzillas who maneuver for repeated social attacks. And how about the employee who thrives on antagonizing his co-workers? Or the habitual complainer or latecomer?

There are a hundred types of offenders out there who undermine and fragment the cohesive work force. These antics test and destroy relationships.

Office politics offer lots of "sides" to take, complete with plenty of gory details, and all kinds of contention and controversy to get sucked into—for what? The issues involved are rarely resolved, so bad feeling is just enhanced when everyone gossips and pursues some sort of jaded revenge. The same principles are true in our families, with neighbors, in the community, or at church.

FORGET AND FORGIVE.

Children seldom have lasting spats in their dealings with each other. But not adults! We have learned to take our disagreements and culture them into lifelong ill feelings.

What damage can holding a longtime grudge or desire to "get even" do for us, even when no one else knows about our feelings?

[DON] *I knew a man who more than once beat me out of large sums of money I'd worked hard to earn. This guy did the same to thirty or more of my fellow contractors. All of us immensely disliked this financial bully, who dishonestly took our money while we took all the losses.*

For ten years I filed this "rat's" name away, watching for an opportunity to get even. One day, word came around (something you think only happens in the movies) that a little collection was being taken up to 'knock off the crook'. At first, a fleeting feeling of pleasure flooded over me. When jolted to my senses I was horrified for even pondering such a thing. But those urges for revenge, trappings of unforgiveness saved up in my mind, had earned interest and acted as an inducement to do something gravely wrong. I was so horrified, I returned home and tore up all of his past due notes I'd been harboring for years. It was the most exhilarating feeling I'd had in months—to forgive and let go of my vengeful attitude.

Successful people don't waste time, energy, or emotion beating up an offender forever. "Keeping score" after the game is over (won or lost) is useless and damaging. Sometimes we can dismiss the whole business and it will generally disarm things. The success-minded get on with the day at hand and don't get hung up on past grievances. Letting unimportant or unalterable matters wash isn't being "chicken"—it is kind, smart and often a relief.

WHEN WE'RE TO BLAME.

When successful people, either intentionally or unintentionally, have caused some battlefield casualties in life's wars, they quickly rectify the rubble. Fixing can start with a simple "I'm truly sorry" said to those wronged. Those three words, when genuine, have fixed more regrettable situations than any others. Instant goodness floods through us when we do this. And we'll be amazed at how creative we can be— finding ways to restore past injuries we've caused to others and ourselves. When sincere restitution is made, those offended or hurt will respect us more and start loving us again. We'll like ourselves better, too.

NURTURE RELATIONSHIPS.

One of our co-workers said, "Ever notice that those who talk and search constantly for meaningful relationships are often the ones who seem to have the fewest?" It's action, not talk alone, that develops good relationships. In other words, *relationships are earned and nurtured, not found.*

You can't put something or somebody on a shelf and call it a relationship. Real relationships also convert responsibility into response. Response is the secret ingredient for great relationships, and it goes both ways.

For years now we've heard Mother's Day talks at church, school, and community events, and every single one of them goes (in one way or another), "I love my mother because she is always there." Being there when we're needed is the key to a successful relationship.

By legal contract we can get allegiance and loyalty, but affection and respect we have to earn.

[DON] *A close friend of mine developed a sudden illness a while ago and died, at age 55. Of course we all rushed to console his widow, offering the usual, "Can I help?"*

She replied with the customary, "Oh, thank you, I'll be fine."

To which we added the perfunctory finishing line, "Well, if there is anything we can do, just call." We left, content that we had extended a loving hand.

My wife understood the importance of real action in this relationship situation and knew most people just don't call back. She learned that family members were coming to the funeral, and the home wouldn't hold them all. So she cleaned up our motor home, put clean sheets on the bed, we gassed it up and delivered it for their use. She didn't just ask, she acted. She saw a need, felt a responsibility, and responded!

To be successful we need to be nice *all the time*, not just when crises appear. Kindness is more effective than judgment or ignoring. There's an element of caring for others before self that's a part of the equation. It's constancy in reaching out beyond our own doors that makes us successful.

[DON] *I was about ten years old when I first remember hearing the word, disposition. Dad bought a new saddle horse for us kids solely on the seller's description: "The horse has a good disposition." This proved to be true—he did what a saddle horse should do—he didn't kick, bite, fight, or buck. He would stop when you fell off, and stand still while you climbed back on. And no matter what the weather was, how many people had climbed on him, or what hill or swamp we steered him to, he always went willingly, never balking or resisting.*

Any of us who can duplicate this horse's disposition will be reasonably far up the ladder of success. Sincerely desiring peace, being on the *inside* the same as we are outwardly and getting along with others for the benefit of all concerned are successful relationship imperatives.

IT'S A TWO-WAY STREET.

To get people interested in us, we have to make ourselves attractive to them, and be genuinely interested in them.

[SANDRA] *We have heard it said, "I <u>appreciate</u> what you do for me, but I <u>love</u> you for what you do for my children." Let me explain by sharing an experience that happened in our family. Paul Anaya is the community computer genius. He has a demanding job, and a large family of his own, but knew my son Roo wanted to learn more about computers. Paul carved time from his schedule and gave my son explanatory books to read, then lists of computer components to buy as he could afford them. The two eventually assembled a computer from scratch as Paul explained things along the way. Now my son is in a position to help others with his own new found skill, all of which began with a neighbor's generous sharing of his own time, coupled with a great attitude.*

Success includes wanting to help others make their life happier or more fulfilled. Attitude and action are close neighbors. If the attitude is sour, there won't be enthusiasm about much of anything, as in this story of a farmer we know, who wasn't interested in making his life or anybody else's happier.

Fred the farmer was a talented man, however he had few friends because basically he was an unhappy, continuous complainer. Nothing could please him entirely and in every conversation you could expect 96% of it to be gripes about the weather, the wind, taxes, traffic, bugs, or his crops. People really hate complainers so they would walk on the other side of the street when they saw old Fred coming. Neighbors even nicknamed his ranch, "Belly-Acres". One year, Fred's potato crop finally came out 100 percent number ones— perfect yield and quality! One neighbor rushed to Fred who was working in the barn and said: "Well Fred… Congratulations! Marvelous! Your whole crop was number ones. Finally you have nothing to complain about."

Fred looked up with his typical frown and grumbled, "Humph, you might know it. No culls [potato rejects] left over to feed my pigs!"

There is an overabundance of Freds around—the chronic complainers who experience the generous perks of life but are always negatively judging and complaining about the government, the roads, restaurants, politics, family, co-workers, sports, weather, and their jobs. They are supported by radio talk show hosts, 99% of whom conduct formalized complaint forums, stirring people up in their irritations without offering good solutions to solve the problems.

Complaining or whining about conditions inside our private life or outside in the world, is unquestionably the prime, single biggest waste of time and emotion of "humanbeinghood." Successful people spend little or no time complaining. They cannot afford to stay irritated. What a sorry pastime to bemoan what's happened. Remembering, expanding, defending or whining about it wastes tons and tons of time.

Everyone likes being around people with a pulse—and few of us can resist people who care. Its no fun to get involved with people who don't get excited over projects…or anything. The "cool dude" is likely cool because he doesn't make sparks at anything.

[DON] *My contracting business, operates in nearly 50 states, and performs maintenance to large commercial buildings like malls, universities, hotels, manufacturing plants, banks, retail chains, etc. Services range from cleaning toilets to maintaining air conditioning, roofs, office partitions, and parking lots. We provide upkeep service, which means our staff needs to be trained in mechanics, public relations, budgeting, safety, security, hiring, handling emergencies and complaints. After years of this training, I've established a three-subject training approach:*

1. *Skill: You've got to know how to do good work*
2. *Speed: You've got to move it*
3. *PR: <u>People have to like you</u>*

The last is the most important of the three because no matter how sharp we are as a mechanic/operator or how fast and efficient we might be at re-tiling the floor, if people don't like us, we cannot perform well enough to please them. The reverse is true, too. If people love and respect us, we can sometimes be a slow klutz and still get promotions!

[SANDRA] *I am acquainted with a bright, middle-aged man who exudes competence in his field. Not a problem comes up that he can't solve. While others appear to muck around and scramble to meet the production and service goals of his company, he lifts himself above the chaos and cuts a straight path to the remedy.*

You'd think a man like this would be indispensable to his firm—but companies also need pleasant, patient personalities probably more than the most brilliant minds. This guy had what we nowadays call a <u>major</u> attitude problem; and he was the only one who couldn't see it.

He felt entitled to more privileges and more homage—perhaps because he was a relative of the owner. Sensitivity to co-worker's feelings or expressing even a minimally charitable attitude was severely lacking. He was sarcastic and demanding and everybody hated to be around him.

One day he was finally asked to leave. Afterward, many of those who worked most closely with him shared that they were immensely relieved. His genius was sacrificed to arrogance as he proved the point that competency can't overcome personality in success.

We've got to continually do things to show we like people; and be likeable ourselves.

There is a hard-core relationships rule: Employment, marriage, and kinship don't ensure success. We have to earn and continually sustain our position through ongoing kindness and sensitivity. Good relationships cannot be inherited or bought. Existence doesn't qualify for acceptance at home or at work. We've got to constantly do things to show we like people, and to be likeable ourselves.

The old "you owe me affection or preference," because "I'm your kid, your spouse, disabled, down on my luck, your employee, depressed, bored, accident-free, clever, or an American..." doesn't work in this life any more than it will work in the next one. People might briefly patronize those demanding types to get them out of the way—but if we plan to endure with anyone or in any company, we better bring something kind to the table—consistently. Successful people both learn and practice this truism.

It is our responsibility to keep ourselves marketable, desirable, productive, and in the loop. Others generally provide the space and the pay for the loop (be it money or affection), but most people won't include us in their overall scheme of things if we don't contribute, offer to help and keep squared away. In a relationship, we generally get what we give. If we are depressed, we are probably depressing. If we *aren't* experiencing quality relationships, maybe we aren't giving any.

TO BUILD RELATIONSHIPS.

GRATITUDE.

Everyone loves getting a *real* note in the snail mail. As soon as we spy that handwritten return address in the upper-left hand corner, we stroke the envelope with a kind of halting reverence. Then comes the ritual of opening it, anxious to see the contents, yet not wanting them to be revealed too quickly...

[SANDRA] *When I sorted through the estate belongings of my recently departed Aunt Martha, I found next to her TV remote, right there in her active everyday space, a collection of opened letters. I fingered through them, noting some postage cancellation dates from more than a decade ago. So I pulled several of the yellowed, ragged-edged letters out of their envelopes and read expressions of appreciation and gratitude, one after another, penned to my aunt for small deeds she had done for these people many years ago. She obviously cherished the thank-you's so much, she stored them right next to her TV chair, for an occasional re-read and morale boost.*

Whether by snail mail, voice mail, or email, sharing a thank you not only says we care—It just makes everybody feel good down deep.

Successful people say thanks, and express appreciation wherever they can. Life is short and thanks are too few.

UNCONDITIONAL LOVE STARTS IN
FAMILY CIRCLES.

Successful families hold relationships together with thousands of tiny threads, not chains. Differences in opinion and lifestyles must be put aside and patience moved to center stage as family members express unconditional love to each other. It is a healthy model to follow for all of our relationships.

As seasoned parents, it seems nearly impossible at times to withhold giving the "expert, full of wisdom" opinions on just about every topic known to our offspring. We reason that they will be advantaged by our insight. It's a slippery situation, balancing parental instruction with parental expectation. Allowing responsible children, as well as our spouses, siblings, friends, co-workers, neighbors, or parents, to have freedom in their personal decisions can be challenging and painful. Relationships move to an excruciating level, challenging tolerance, when our loved ones don't measure up to our standards, or when they purposely defy our own moral maps.

No one is an expert on how to relate to another. "I know just how you feel" is almost a laugh. We can easily over or underestimate what others think, do, or feel. Psychologists claim to predict personality types, but who of us really knows the inner workings of even our nearest and dearest's mind? No judgments can be perfect as we analyze each other. So we must operate from a rather restricted base, which, when you think about it, makes our best guesses quite risky.

[SANDRA] *I attended the funeral of a friend who had been an esteemed accountant in the community. He had hundreds of clients who all loved and respected him. An exacting man by nature, he had apparently carried his perfectionist ideals into his personal life, to excess. At the service, I was surprised to learn that one of his sons had been estranged from him for many years simply because he had grown his hair long. The father disapproved of this. I was told it wasn't until he was lying on his deathbed, that the two finally reconciled the standoff. Years of opportunity for showing affection had been lost due to intolerance on the father's part and defiance from the son.*

It is not unusual for associations to be weakened because two points of view clash. If we want successful relationships, our personal *preferences* must not become more important than weightier *principles*—in this case, unconditional love.

What determines our acceptance of people? Do we make too big a deal of dress, education, body size, clean rooms, past offenses or even hairstyles? No matter how cleverly, subtly or smoothly we serve up our opinions, others may bristle. Loving unconditionally means caring more about the relationship than about being *right*.

COMMON things successful people do to show unconditional acceptance of others.

- Read and personally respond to letters, gifts, notes, pictures
- Help other people's children with anything
- Invite people to go special places with you—even send them tickets
- Give photos (make enlarged copies from prints)
- Visit them when they're sick or down
- Offer family and childcare help
- Acknowledge the value of their pets and hobbies
- Write a poem for them
- Share home-grown and home-cooked foods
- Offer appropriate help

Simply caring for someone is a cold responsibility in a relationship, but loving someone is true passion. Heartfelt goodwill is what motivates us to nurture relationships. There is nothing like knowing and feeling we are really going *some*where, doing *some*thing, and sharing a vision with *some*one. This is the ultimate toilet-free path to well-being and success.

Successful People Keep the Rules

Sometimes we, the *intelligent* species on this planet, do things that would be funny if they weren't almost pathetic.

We sing and pray for brotherhood, but decorate the park right across the street from the church with cannons, retired warplanes, and other monuments to destruction. We say we love our fellow man, but the number of lawsuits grows by leaps and bounds.

We over-exercise because we've over-eaten. We lay down our pipe to shake a fist at our kids for smoking too young and we yell at our spouses for screaming at our children. We vow to die for our country and what she stands for, but rape her resources and litter her highways daily. We wouldn't miss a single movie or Super Bowl game featuring the entertainers and heroes we worship; yet only two percent of us visit our kid's schools in a year, where future leaders of government and commerce are being forged.

[DON] *My earliest, and by far most significant experience with rules and law, came from the U.S. Forest Service and the Idaho department of Fish and Game. As a youth, hunting, fishing, and camping meant uncles, aunts, and cousins coming together. It was a joyful time, generally taking place in Forest Service territory or under it's supervision. They set most of the boundaries, hours and limits to keep order and preserve nature. There were campfire rules, daylight and nighttime regulations, opening and closing season days— all of these set down to protect nature and keep us "users" from shooting, drowning, and* wasting each other.

What stands out in my memory was not the rules themselves; it was the amount of effort some of my uncles and their friends took to out-fox the "law". My father insisted that poachers, without exception, were thieves—even an extra single fish or pheasant over the limit was a heinous crime. Yet my uncles seemed so clever in how to "fool" the game wardens. They would shoot or catch way over the limit then find a way to hide the illegal bounty to pass through the checking station. This seemed so adventuresome, these 101 ways to beat the law and try to outwit the big forest ranger. I remember them laughing at how they smuggled two extra pheasants through the checkpoint by hiding them under my Aunt's dress so she appeared pregnant. I recall my uncle once crying the blues about how he hid several quail in the hubcaps of his car (clever man). It was the perfect crime until Trigger, the Irish setter, jumped out of the car and went directly to the rear tire and proceeded to "set" the "pointer pose" at the hubcap. This showed the ranger where to find the illegal game and enabled the state to levy a fat fine. Good people—but in their eyes getting caught was the crime, not doing something illegal. If they got away with it, it was okay.

For years, the Fourth of July meant loss of fingers, eyes, and huge fires all caused by fireworks. Finally, "Seize and Containment Laws" were created to limit the kind and amount of amateur explosives that could be used in Idaho— but the illegal variety of fireworks was still available across the border in Wyoming. So after church, a good family would load into the car, drive a few miles, and spend a small fortune on a stash—hide them under a blanket and drive home. Later, they slithered off to a private spot and set them off. Most fires, wrecks, injuries and drownings result from disobeying or ignoring a rule.

Some of the best men and women we know are or were "in the toilet" because they got into a position of power, wealth, and influence and deemed themselves exempted or above the law—letting leverage replace logic.

We shell out thousands in taxes to hire police and other public officers to help keep us safe and secure and protect us from bad things. Then we buy books and devices, and spend hours in conversation and at seminars learning how we can outthink these guardians, sidestepping the very safety we are paying for.

We devise and perfect games for the pleasure of competing, setting boundaries and rules to keep things fair and fun. Then we give little "Johnny Klutz" six strikes instead of three and tarnish the game for all the other seven-year-olds who play by the rules.

We toss warranties and directions the minute we open the box or drive out of the showroom, just expecting things to work because we own them. Then we discover our new toy is ruined because we did the very thing "page 2" warned us not to do.

A fuzz buster (radar detector) in our car is there for one reason- to serve as a technical aid for breaking the law. If we aren't speeding, we don't need one. A fuzz buster is an overt declaration that we choose not to obey the same law we pledge to obey and pay for.

Bottom line, successful people get ahead in life by keeping and living the rules.

INCLINATION TO BREAK THE RULES.

Haven't we all met "Mr. Good Guy" who finds challenge and intrigue in *beating the system*—not really an outright criminal but a rule bender, limit tester, just-for-the-fun-of-it person? He sees a questionable rule and feels this overwhelming inclination to get past it some way. He delights when he can beat the cross arm signal at a railroad crossing, get a little over the load limit, snatch a bigger portion than he paid for, or defy curfew.

[DON] *I remember well, when I was ten or eleven, the milk truck driver for our route. He was an exciting personality whose schedule at one point was timed perfectly with the morning Express. He took pride as he beat the train to the crossing even if he had to break lots of little traffic laws to do it. He was our community icon. How daring and clever he was. Then, one morning it was a disastrous tie! Milk cans and Dave were strewn down the track for a quarter mile.*

When Dave's widow was asked why she thought he found so much delight in breaking the rules to reach the crossing first, she had some ready answers that can probably be generalized to all of us at some point,

- He took it as a challenge
- He had a "thing" about authority
- He loved the attention
- He was a competitor

Bottom line, Dave could revel in his glory for a time, but he couldn't revel in his grave. Ironically, every rule he broke existed to protect him and keep him alive.

NICE GUYS MIGHT FINISH LAST.

In spite of our knowledge and acceptance that the rules are for the good of most of us, we still find a space to grieve at the seeming injustice when bad rule-breaking guys get good results. Many of those who cheat and lie their way through school seem as good or better off than the "honest" folks. The gal on the block who doesn't help diddley in community, church, or with youth has equal or better clothes, cars, and kids. The guy who leaves his matronly wife for a younger woman seems to be happy and rewarded. The colleague who bribed his way into a political position is sure more popular than you or me. What's the deal here?

Must little guys always finish last?

What is our incentive to keep the rules when apparent dishonest or compromising short cuts have worked so well for so many? Solomon, a biblical hero to many, gives some insight to this apparent unfairness issue when he said, because *a sentence against an evil work is not executed speedily,* it's embedded in our hearts to do evil. Even so, laws and rules are not on trial—they eventually work for us. Our incentive to keep rules is simply freedom. Freedom from,

- Personal anxiety
- Legal arrest
- Colleagues mistrust
- God and Nature's consequences

[DON] *I was in a physiology class taking my final exam when my teacher got an emergency call and slipped out for the last minute of the test. Answers for the questions ricocheted around the room. Oh yes! I recognized the ones I'd forgotten now. I thought over the advantage I'd been given but laid down my pencil. A notch up on a grade scale wasn't worth the price to get it.*

> *We hope to never be caught, but when we knowingly break any rule, one of the dispensers of eventual justice—others, nature, the legal system, the Creator, or ourselves—will eventually prevail.*

We can't go anywhere or buy anything without words or pages of printed matter warning of what will happen if we ignore rules. The successful don't skip over these things, waiting for the slap on the side of the head, the lawsuit, the broken machinery, the heart attack, or the accident.

[DON] *Several years ago, we paid our entry fee at the gate to Yellowstone Park and were given a handful of literature including maps and Park rules. The bright yellow warning sheet amused us. It was so direct and blunt we asked, "Who would ever be dumb enough to approach a one-ton wild beast like a buffalo anyway?"*

Less than two miles down the road we rounded a turn and a little meadow opened before us. Scores of cars were parked just off the road. People with dangling cameras and poor judgment were creeping toward (you guessed it) a herd of buffalo.

The more sensible members of the families, mostly women and children, remained safely near their cars, futilely waving the yellow warning sheets. But the determined novice photographers (men) with their ultra-latest digital camcorders drew confidence from each other. In aggressive unity they inched across the meadow, each competing with the next to move into closer range of the grazing bison.

We drove off before the situation boiled over, shaking our heads in disbelief. How could any of our fellow humans be so stupid? Putting yourself within tromping range of huge, deadly, hooked-horned creatures just to photograph them doesn't make sense.

Pretty soon you could expect to hear the sound of an ambulance echo through the trees. Someone didn't outrun the buffalo.

WARNING

NATIONAL PARK SERVICE

MANY VISITORS HAVE BEEN GORED BY BUFFALO

BUFFALO CAN WEIGH 2000 POUNDS AND CAN SPRINT AT 30 MPH, THREE TIMES FASTER THAN YOU CAN RUN

THESE ANIMALS MAY APPEAR TAME BUT ARE WILD, UNPREDICTABLE, AND DANGEROUS

DO NOT APPROACH BUFFALO

Seldom, very seldom, can we truly say, "I didn't know." Sure we knew—there was a big picture or sign, a siren, or even a loudspeaker warning us of impending danger; just like that big buffalo-warning sheet with a cartoon of a tourist being bashed and thrashed.

Ambulance-beckoning behaviors are always shunned by the successful.

[SANDRA] *My acquaintance up the street brags to everyone about how he sails right past the stop sign by his house on the way to work each morning. He claims he's never had a ticket or accident. But how many more times will he beat the system ...or has he really been beating it?*

Exceptions to the rules, or evasions of them, are usually a delayed invitation to disaster. We can run a stop sign or ignore a warning sign once, or maybe even twenty times, without a hint of a problem. But the collision will come if we keep making exceptions to a rule long enough.

RULES.

[DON] *"My manager, an experienced pilot for our southern district, was stationed in Atlanta to supervise operations in the Carolinas and Florida. This gave him reason to fly a twin Piper private plane. Always a little nervous about what could happen to small planes, I was constantly full of questions, which he always confidently answered.*

On one blue-sky trip, I asked him what would happen if he saw a plane coming head-on toward him. "Never happens," he said, "We fly opposite directions with 1000 foot elevation differences; that's the rule." Then he confidently added, "If it should happen, the rule is when we see each other, we both veer instantly to our right, becoming totally safe." Flying home that day it happened. We spotted a tiny dot quickly

growing bigger, exactly on our altitude, directly in our line of flight. In seconds we identified it as another private plane clipping along at 200 m.p.h. like us. My manager sharply veered to the right but the oncoming plane veered to her left and we swished past each other too close to call. A near mid-air collision!

Successful people have faith in the rules. They know rules keep people alive, safe, efficient and free *if they are followed.*

THE UNCAUGHT COUNTS TOO!

A guest on an early morning TV talk show was founder and president of the organization MADD (Mother's Against Drunk Drivers). A twenty-eight-year-old man, who'd just killed two youngsters while driving intoxicated, joined her. He said, in his defense, "Well, it was my first offense."

The mother (whose teen daughter had been killed by another drunk driver) said, "No sir, it wasn't likely your first offense. It was the first time you were caught. Studies show that drunk drivers have one arrest for every twenty times they are actually drinking and driving."

The uncaught in life counts and it will play catch-up at the worst possible time. Successful people don't scheme to avoid getting seized. They know that when laws are obeyed there's simply never an opening for a slip into the toilet.

Justice may be a slow punisher, but it's a sure one. Have you ever done something wrong and feared getting nailed for it? Suddenly we're sure we've been discovered and we're terrified—not to mention mad at ourselves. We make sudden vows and earnest pledges that if just this once we could be passed over, we will have learned our lesson and never do it again.

In the midst of our deepest guilt and punishment preview, we realize it was a false alarm. No one found us out. We're relieved, exuberant – just like taking off an overcoat in a steam room. We offer a quick prayer of thanks for having been spared, but then put the black hat right back on again. It fits even more securely now and we wear it with arrogance. After all, almost getting caught or hurt surely must improve our odds of never getting caught or hurt.

A certain bookkeeper decided that with a slight adjustment of one little amount she could free up enough money to get herself a foothold, a nest egg— and then she would put her dishonesty to rest.

When no one caught on, her confidence increased and she got bolder and bolder. She helped herself to a little more here and there, and eventually she was on the wrong side of the law, big time. Now she's got one of those precision stainless steel toilets that matches the decor of her entry door.

Larceny

Oh, Curse that bit of larceny
We all have in our souls,
We are 99% honest folks
but that 1% sure pulls.

Perhaps it's just a "one up"
By means of skullduggery
After all an extra coin or two
Is not a felony!

Advantages, or more than earned
Might tip into our favor,
A little unearned praise or cash
Certainly we can savor!

Surely we would not steal
Or practice thievery,
But oversight, of what's not right
We'll accept it silently.

When we gain an inch of ground
On the darker side of sly,
If no one sees, and no one cares
Tis' surely not a lie.

Oh, curse that bit of larceny
We all have in our souls,
We are 99% honest folks…
But that 1% still shows!

HOW ABOUT WE MAKE OUR OWN RULES?

We never thought much about rules or laws growing up. They were just there. The government had some, God had some, the school had some, each sport had some, and parents had some. To get along with people, you followed the rules.

Then came college and classes that had a way of moving us toward free thought, free love, and liberation. Now there was the possibility of making our own rules to custom fit us, which some students did.

Surely these students were smarter than our founding fathers, the medical profession, the coach, and the police. They were their own personal rulers, philosophers, and lawmakers.

At first, many of their new rules seemed perfect, but after a while these folks got tangled up in some serious consequences. Most of those with ultra-contemporary attitudes about marriage were divorced. Those who didn't believe in disciplining children were heartsick. All who ate, drank, or sniffed bad stuff were ill, fat, in prison, or dead from it.

One morning in social science class a freethinking, bold intellectual in the back of the room challenged the rules, saying,

"Well, I just don't accept that new lower speed limit for driving on the Interstate. I didn't make the law, so why do I have to obey it? It should be my choice as an American, to do it or not to do it." The class chortled with admiration for this brazen assertion against the law.

The teacher reminded him, "Wilson, there are punishments and consequences for breaking the rules."

"I don't accept them either," he muttered. The teacher then challenged Wilson to a little experiment.

"You're the speeder and I'm the judge," she said. The class was delighted to watch Wilson take on the teacher. She tossed on a make-believe judge's robe and Wilson was led before her.

"Mr. Wilson, you were caught doing 95 in a 55 m.p.h. zone, how do you plead?"

"Guilty, judge because I can drive any speed I like, that's my option." (The class clapped.)

The judge banged the gavel on the bench. "Then I sentence you to be taken out and hung by the neck until dead!"

Wilson sarcastically retorted, "Sorry, you can't hang me judge. The most that can happen is I get a $100 fine and go free."

The class applauded.

"But Mr. Wilson, like you, I believe in options and I don't have to obey the law or rules either. I can sentence you to anything I want. And I feel like sentencing you to die for speeding!"

Wilson gasped. He'd hung himself with his freedom of speech and logic. He'd never considered that rules and laws were for his protection, too.

Someone once said, "We often get so caught up in our rights, we forget what *is* right." Laws and rules are meant to provide some kind of social balance for us all. Even if *some* seem unfair to *some* of us *some* of the time, the laws are meant for the general welfare of all the citizens, not just our own at any given time.

Successful people are rule-followers. But if they reach a point where they feel they are finally exempt from the rules, they quickly become unsuccessful. We read about folks like these every day in the "toilet" sections of the newspaper.

We've watched rich, politically powerful, and athletically talented people lose everything (friends, health, job, etc.) because they grew to believe they were exempt from the rules.

One example of this is the tragic story of basketball superstar Len Bias. He excelled in basketball at the high school and college levels. After many years of hard work and preparation, Len was ready to make the jump to the pros. He was the number two player selected in the 1986 NBA draft, chosen by the Boston Celtics—considered to be one of the greatest basketball teams of all time. On June 19, 1986, Len Bias signed a multi-million dollar contract. The following morning, Bias died of a Cocaine overdose.

Tax laws, traffic laws, drinking laws, national forest laws and moral laws apply to all successful people.

While we were putting together this chapter of rules that we commonly break, we quickly agreed that if a soda machine yielded a free can, most people would probably leave the equivalent

Successful people learn to follow rules long before consequences demand it!

money behind—yet these same folks may construct building additions without permits. The same people who never cheat a penny on their taxes—are willing to loan a personal ski pass to a colleague so they can beat the system.

Some use the company mail system to stamp and send personal letters, yet believe fuzz busters are immoral. Some lend their driver licenses to out-of-state friends to give them a "resident" advantage. Or maybe claim their three-year-old child is actually only two, to avoid purchasing a full-fare airline ticket. Most friends we talked with admit to occasionally sneaking outside food into show houses to avoid paying for high-priced theater concessions, or using their cell-phone in restricted places. But these same people said it's wrong to turn back the odometer on a used car they were selling.

Here are some RULES even the most "law-abiding" of us often ignore or bend. How does breaking them affect our ultimate success?

Put a check mark by those *you* break—

❑ Fail to report income, or declare questionable deductions on income tax
❑ Pad (and stretch) expense accounts and use the company vehicle credit card to pay for personal gas
❑ Airline rules: sneak on extra suitcases or carry-ons; fudge about kid's ages
❑ Strain to get the senior citizen discount prematurely
❑ Copy videotapes or computer programs despite all those big warnings
❑ Sneak an extra bite or two of food to members of your dinner group who did not pay for the buffet

❑ Dump excess trash into the neighbor's trash cans
❑ Sneak an extra person or persons into the motel room
❑ At hospitals, support patient's bad habits by bringing in forbidden rich foods, cigarettes, a shot of whiskey, whatever.
❑ And as American as the Fourth of July: get and set off illegal fireworks, the bigger the better!
❑ Ignore the road detour and skirt around barricades
❑ Fail to get Fido his license
❑ Ignore drought restrictions against watering lawns, etc.
❑ Turn back the odometer on the golden oldie we are about to sell
❑ Litter the highway

TRAFFIC LAWS:
❑ Drive 5-10 or so miles over the limit
❑ Make a U-turn where we're not supposed to, if we're in a hurry
❑ Slow down, rather than stop, at stop signs
❑ Ignore those signs that say "Local traffic only"
❑ Only slow down a little for school zones
❑ Park across several spaces, or in a handicapped zone
❑ Forget to wear seat belts
❑ Ignore "for customers only" notices on lavatory doors at restaurants, gas stations and stores that we are not patronizing.

WORK PROBLEMS:

❏ Take supplies home from work
❏ Make personal copies on the company machine
❏ Use the mailroom for personal mail
❏ Personal use of the office telephone
❏ Use of Internet to surf for private purposes
❏ Fudge on the time card
❏ Use "sick leave" for absences that are not health-related.
❏ Refuse to wear any kind of safety gear—safety glasses, respirators, helmets, hairnets, etc. Too much trouble, or too unflattering.

❏ A biggee—the marriage vows (to love, honor, and obey, let alone the one about being faithful)

EXEMPT

*When I perceive and start to believe
That rules are for the other guys,
That what they can't be, is OK for me
And I'm judged through different eyes.*

*The laws of health,
the order of wealth,
For me there is every excuse.
Fidelity too. Why, that's for you!
I'm happy because I'm loose.*

*Now if I slip, hand or lip,
There is always a reason why.
Exception clause, I'm beyond the laws
That to the others apply.*

*The bad that could be
won't happen to me,
I'm free to tread life's garden.
I'm clearly above the rules of love
For my stumble there's always
a pardon.*

Oh, Really!

*It's an error indeed to
think we won't bleed,
For action not up to code.
For we all win or lose,
from just how we choose,
And eventually pack our own load.*

THE FUDGE FACTOR.

[DON] *I remember well when I learned the real meaning of the word fudge. I'd never heard it (except as a name for candy) until 5th grade at Sugarloaf School. Our old building held all eight grades in one room.*

It was spring and marbles were the in-thing, much like computer games and internet today. There was no age or size discrimination. All kids played together to win or lose their marbles.

One day I was in a deadly serious game and just made a critical shot with my best marble. The bully of the school yelled, "fudge, fudge!" which meant I'd leaned over the line while making my shot. I was horrified at the call—but it stuck. Fudging automatically disqualified you—so he scooped up my prize marble and left.

The boundary line was the shooting line and any fudging, accidental or not, put you in the loser's circle quick.

Years later, while I was submitting a bid on a government installation, someone in the conference asked the official present, "What is the fudge factor?" In other words, how much on either side of the line can we go without getting caught or fined?

*The government man was insulted in front of all those contractors. With the greatest dignity he said something I always remembered, "Ladies and gentlemen, there **is** no fudge factor."*

If we could all manage to live a no fudge line standard, we'd be in a lot less tangle.

TO TELL THE TRUTH.

Many of us *embellish* things like our gas mileage, sex life, the extent of the accident, kid's achievements, savings amounts, incomes, investments, results of doctor visits and surgeries, the size of the spider we just killed or the length of the fish we caught. But we tend to *down play* the traffic ticket, how much the new car set us back, how much we spend eating out and on clothes, how much sleep we got the night before and the amount of food we eat (and our weight along with it).

We have a strong tendency to report things as being much worse or much better than they actually are because we thrive on either sympathy or praise. We want to be martyrs or heroes in the eyes of others—whichever brings us the most notice. If we tell our commonplace experiences and relate what really happened, we get ignored. Here we get our training from the media. The sensational makes it to the screen—average goes unacknowledged.

For a time, people pay more attention to us if our daily happenings are more out of the ordinary. Thus, we work to be uniquely positive or negative—but at least mysterious or different enough to be noticed.

The successful circle of people is not pushed to embellish things hoping to be singular. They are content with truthful, exact reporting. Their confidence is not bolstered by notice—it is fortified by exactness.

IT MAY BE LEGAL,
BUT IS IT MORAL?

Legality is a set of rules trying to regulate society, but only morality can determine right. Legally, it may be okay to leave a room at school, a motel, or home in a mess. It is not illegal to break training rules or ignore the handicapped, but is it moral? It may be legal to wriggle out of an agreement on a technicality, and you can sometimes legally ignore commitments. Surely there are four hundred ways to legally steal. None is right or moral, even though legal.

SOME HONESTY TESTS TO THINK ABOUT.

✔ You schedule a van to pick you up at LAX airport at 6:00 PM. It will cost $30.00 for the trip from there to the hotel. You arrive early and proceed to the van pick-up area at 5:30 PM. There sits a new plush van from another company. They offer to take you right then and there for $25.00.
What are you going to do? Take the van at hand, or wait for the van that you promised your business to?

✔ You get a good deal on a computer table for the office. Your boss is expecting to pay $200.00 cash but you purchase it for $150.00. At the same time, you also pick up a $30.00 case of paper for yourself. *Do you simply add it to the computer table bill?*

✔ Your company allows you $175.00 per day to cover motel and eating expenses. However, it turns out you can sleep and eat at your brother's house for free and avoid spending any of the company's money. *Do you submit a $175.00 voucher and keep the money? Give it back? Give it to your brother?*

✔ At the end of the year, while figuring your income tax... you have all of your 1090's and W-2's stating your income. However, you did get a sizable check for selling a car (that you had previously deducted and depreciated) amounting to $5,000. There is no way the IRS can find out about this sale because you were paid in cash. *Do you report it?*

✔ You are a guitar player and see an ad in a newspaper for a used guitar. Upon arriving at the address of the seller, you discover that the owner is an 81-year-old, poor lady. Her husband has recently passed away and she is selling some of his old stuff, including this

(continued...)

aged instrument. She then shows you the guitar and you realize that it is a Martin D-21, easily worth $3-4,000 dollars. You cordially ask her how much she wants for it, and she replies, "Is $50 is asking too much?" *What do you pay?*

✔ A young mom finishes her grocery shopping and wheels her cart out to the car to unload it. Then she straps two toddlers into their car seats and is surprised to find that the second one had grabbed a 12-pack of triple A batteries at the checkout stand. *Does she reload the kids back into the cart and return the batteries? Does she pay for or return them on her next visit or keep them, rationalizing that the store shouldn't have placed them within a toddler's reach?*

✔ Does our response to make a refund right depend on whether we are under or overcharged?

Bankruptcy was originally intended to help people who, through no fault or indulgence of their own, came upon a crisis or insurmountable circumstance and could not pay their debts. Now it is often just a legal way to escape moral obligations. Legality is a guideline; morality *is* the line. Every one of our poorly chosen actions, even legal ones, carry over into the rest of our lives. Just like spitting into a strong head wind, they return to make us feel like we got blown backward into a toilet.

Successful people aren't forever trying to find all the angles and loopholes and legal ways to beat the system. And they don't assess situations solely on issues of legality. They know that their conscience is more accurate than any law book and they listen to it—and obey.

PLAYING BY THE RULES !

Isn't it amazing how smoothly games run when we all play by the same rules? If we do have a dispute the umpire or referee with the help of a rulebook can easily resolve it. When we bypass perimeters, we've opened up the toilet lid and we're trifling with getting "rear-ended."

Don't get us wrong, successful people blaze plenty of their own trails in life, but they do it within the boundaries that are set up to protect them and others. It's an inarguable fact that when we reach a certain age in America we do have the right to do just about anything we want, (age 21, alcohol; age 18, tobacco; age 17, R-rated movies) anywhere we want, and whenever we want. We have freedom of choice to make some of our own rules if we don't like those of God, the nation, the workplace, or the doctor. But we better be ready to accept the consequences.

Someone once said that most rules and laws were made in wisdom and thoughtfulness after years of experiment in the laboratory of life.

Not just God, but human societies,

successful doctors, lawyers, engineers, teachers, financial experts, chemists, biologists, farmers, and parents have contributed to the rules. Building codes, safety rules, manufacturing standards, load limits, loan ratios, driving regulations, prescription doses, swimming pool chlorine dilutions, and even kitchen recipes *are all tested and set up to help make our everyday living experiences successful.* They save us money, time, emotional drain, and bad consequences.

The successful people we know don't lie, sneak, adjust, dilute, bribe, bend, ignore, or exaggerate for their convenience and benefit – sucking them into a toilet situation.

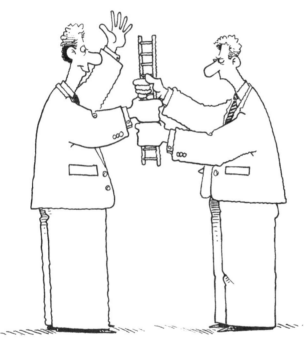

Isn't it amazing how smoothly the game goes when we all play by the same rules?

Successful People Make the Most of Time

Generally we look at the hundreds of choices that occur in our normal living as exclusively moral, emotional, economic, or political decisions. But they are also very much decisions of *Time*. Consider the following,

Hold on! I'm still smelling!

ROSE GARDEN

THE VCR:
It's old, it's temperamental, and it's marginal. Do we fix it or fling it?

THE CAR
It runs, but is getting scary. Do we repair or replace it?

THE DOG
She is old and has arthritis, but the kids still love her. Do we put her to sleep or take her to the vet, again and again?

THE HIP
Is so bad it is getting painful to walk. Is it surgery or suffer?

THE NEIGHBOR
Wants to do battle over common street parking. Do we fight it or forget it?

THE TICKET
We got for illegal parking is unfair. Do we challenge it or let it wash?

Perhaps property, money, and status are not among our most important holdings as we are usually taught. Rather, with enough *time* we can have or do just about anything. It is "time shortage" that is the focus of most of our efforts.

Deciding whether to save a marginally functioning air conditioner or a marginally functioning marriage really isn't a wallet call; it is a time call—the willingness to spend the time (which governs effort and money) to fix it. When confronted with any "decision call" we have the choice to *fight against it, ignore it, delay it* or *follow through* and fix it. Some of us will immediately jump on the situation, deeming it of great importance to resolve; others will literally ignore it, not wanting to spend the effort.

Celebrating birthdays, for example, has little or no significance to some people. They forget or *ignore* them, and often do not even acknowledge the event for themselves. Conversely others *follow through* and go nearly berserk, with big efforts, days off and parties at every opportunity. Either of these approaches represents a *time* cost. Is the outcome worth the time it will take? Do we fight against, ignore, delay, or follow through? This is an extremely big issue for those who want to keep their lives out of the toilet.

Everything we encounter—little glitches, errors, and challenges, can be expanded or whisked away. Our reaction to nearly every happening represents an investment of time. For example, a seemingly minor, unattended cut could get infected and we could lose a limb or a life because we ignored it. But we reason that most of these cuts self-heal instead of get worse, so the time it would take to see a doctor greatly influences our decision. Menial and precious calls in life are all important, because either way time is passing and consequences result.

The ever-popular nursery rhyme about lost sheep (or keys, a shoe, purse, whatever) reminds us that Bo Beep had a time decision to make.

Little Bo Peep has lost her sheep
And doesn't know where to find them.
Leave them alone, they will come home,
Wagging their tails behind them.

She decided to ignore her problem for the time being. But she had other time choices that we seldom talk about. When her sheep showed up missing she could blame someone else, make a mountain out of a molehill, stare at the hillside, call 911, sue her fence company, madly drive the neighborhood in her suburban looking for them, submit an insurance claim, or demand Shepherd Workman's Compensation.

Many things we shouldn't slough off, but some things can and should be for the sake and value of time. We seldom see a successful person involved in the petty pile up of peripheral happenings, or as someone wise once explained, they do not get caught in the "thick of thin things." Let's take our five target areas of life's traffic, and look at their time implications.

How do we respond when…
RELATIONSHIPS
We hear them say something bad about us
They forget our birthday two years in a row
Someone swears in a public place
Some jerk crowds a line we've been waiting in
They take our parking place
We find out our spouse cheated on us

We get a hate letter from a friend
The neighbors are noisy

RULES
We forget to report $75.00 to I.R.S.
We get a speeding ticket for driving 75 in a 45 m.p.h. zone, (we were really only doing 72 m.p.h..)
They raise property taxes again
A neighbor is using drugs
The group doesn't get a valid permit to march on Saturday
They make the street in front of our house a one-way
Someone has thirty items in the ten items or less food line at the grocery store
Our 80-year-old mother refuses to wear the seat belt in our car

TIME
Our flight is late
The people at work constantly stop and chat five to ten minutes
They move our favorite TV show from 7:30 am to 11:30 PM
There is a two-hour wait in the ticket line to see a concert
Service is slow at a high-priced restaurant
We finally get in at 3:30 PM for our doctor's 2:00 PM appointment
Traffic is a creeping parking lot
Dandelions are all over the lawn

HEALTH
The wrong order of food comes in the restaurant
Someone eats the frosting off the corner of the cake

Dogs bark all night and keep us awake
We have shortness of breath and chest
pain
Our usual allergies act up
They add caffeine to our favorite root
beer
Our company requires a physical

MONEY
We get home and find we were short-
changed
Our spouse overdraws the account, again
We don't get the promised raise
Credit card interest goes up
We hear that our neighbor is making
more than we are
We realize ball players are overpaid
Our friends have a real deal for sure
(network marketing)
We buy the new mower one week before
the 50%-off sale begins
The house we sold for $80,000 just re-
sells for $280,000

The average person might get hung
up, bugged, or bent out of shape on
most of these, while the wise and
successful approach might be to briefly
acknowledge most of them but only *fix*
three or four on the whole list of forty
time-takers. Most things, if forgiven,
will self-heal in time.

AFTER THE DECISION TO DO IT.

Time <u>still</u> is a factor even after we
make the right call to fix or pursue
something. How *much* time should we
give, use, spend? There is a factor of

diminishing returns that applies not only
to money, but also to time.

For example, we decide to host the
picnic on July 4th. Is it better to use hard
or paper plates? We go for the paper.
Their convenience and appropriateness
supercedes the spending; our time is
worth more than our money. We decide
it's a good call.

Let's take a quick look at five other
common time-value calls.

CELEBRATIONS—
The night we attend the big event—
how much time do we spend driving,
parking, standing in line and fighting
traffic? Is it worth it?

EXERCISE—
This is necessary but we must like
still use judgment. If we spend five years
at it, and it helps us live 10 years longer,
has it been worthwhile?

CLEANING—
Does it need to be done daily?
Weekly? Monthly? There is always dust.
The level of cleanliness is based totally
on how often we clean, but is the time
spent worth the appearance?

SHOPPING—
We drive to four different shopping
centers and save four dollars? How do
we weigh $4.00 against four hours of
time?

GROOMING—

It makes us all feel better and look better. Is it worth doing fifteen minutes a morning or two hours, knowing that both the time and looks are gone by the end of the day?

EATING—

We love to try the new recipes in Bon Appetit. It takes time to shop for the unusual ingredients as well as the cookware to prepare it in. Is the pleasure of the final product worth the hours of preparation time?

Are there any criterion (besides good sense) to help us make the call of when to walk away or tackle the situation?

One person put together his own little choosing chart and we have learned much from it…

I FORGET IT WHEN…	I PURSUE IT WHEN…
It will hurt others	It helps others
I see a dead end	I see progress
It is unenjoyable	It's going to be exciting
It will self-destruct	I know it won't go away until fixed
It's overall unprofitable	It's overall profitable
Wise counsel says "no"	Wise counsel says "yes"

WHEN IT'S TIME TO RECONSIDER.

Confusing stubbornness (refusing to yield) with persistence (refusing to give-up) is a guaranteed misery maker. It happens to us all occasionally—we think something is a good idea, pursue it for a while, and find out it's not coming out like we imagined. Then we start struggling with it, instead of just backing up and adjusting our strategy. Or we stick to something and hit what we aimed for, but we aimed wrong. Then instead of just admitting it wasn't a good idea, we aim at that same target again, and compound the undesirable results.

An error? Mistake? Misjudgment? It happens to the smartest of us, and if we have an ounce of ambition, it's likely to happen again and again

in our lives. When it does, do we stand and fight the outcome, determined to make our bad plan work, or do we disengage and redesign?

"Bloom where we are planted" is good advice in general. But not when we've dug ourselves a winding furrow in infertile soil. The best preparation, planning, and execution cannot make a bad idea good. We aren't obligated to dwell where things aren't good. "Sticking with it," when we're pretty sure the outcome isn't what we're after, is stubborn—stupid, to be exact. No matter how long we've worked to get somewhere or something, it can turn out to be sour, not what we wanted, expected, or needed—totally uncomfortable and unworkable. We can dig in and do battle for more months and years, or we can admit that we misjudged, measure again, and march off in a different direction.

We've seen people quit school, jobs, marriage, and service, to literally tend their struggles. They create a time and place where they can take their woes and devote full time to them. They get so far into tending bad decisions that they let everything else go—like relationships, church, hobbies, exercise, and decent eating.

TROUBLED TIMES.

Struggles come even when we don't create them for ourselves. The merry-go-round of life won't stop to unload just because our hands are tired of holding on. We simply have to manage

to get a better grip on the rod. We've learned we don't have to interrupt the flow of anything while struggling. During our bluest time we *can often* make our brightest moves. We can walk while wounded—even run. We can keep climbing with a sore heart and bloody hands. Launching something new and big and challenging can actually be the best remedy for troubled times. When our goals fall into the toilet, it's really dumb to pour all of our time and

We can often accomplish the most during our hardest struggles.

emotion into that container of life. Keep the other forty containers of life active —something few people realize they can and should do. We come upon a hardship and instead of backing up and taking the large view of things, we go to bed with the burden and close our eyes to everything else. We may be overdrawn, losing a family member, or hit with that arthritis again, but the kids still have to be sent off to school, the soul and spirit nourished, and the paid bills dropped in the mailbox. Struggling shouldn't eliminate progress—we don't stop pushing and pulling and progressing because we have a problem. Some people sit around and try to overcome a problem and do nothing else. If by a miracle they do get it all worked out, in their time away from the front lines of living, a thousand new enemy weeds have grown up, creating 20 new struggles.

DOES TIME RUN OUT?

Some people say, "Take your time!" but we don't have it to take. No one owns time. We only have the use of it.

"I never had the time" is invalid.

"It's about time!" is too late.

"Is this a bad time?" is our call only.

"Behind time," is lost.

"Time out," doesn't exist.

Success takes time—the intelligent, sacred, careful use of it. How often do we wonder where some people seem to get all their time? They just seem to have it—plenty of it! No matter where, when, or how busy they are, they "find time". It's astonishing! One of their secrets—*they use the time most of us let slip by.* If we ever think we'll run out of time, we're not thinking success. Everyone has time to be successful and happy and should allow no time to be in the toilet, especially waiting for something to get better.

IS "TOO BUSY" BAD?

No! How many times have we heard (or said), referring to someone who is down, discouraged, and struggling, "Harry, you are trying to do too much." There is a myth here that a busy schedule is a killer, and that when life goes in the toilet, it is because we have "too much to do." Careful! This is seldom a valid assumption. It is more often the unbusy, unscheduled people who are under-productive, and unhappy. Piled-on work seldom smothers; it mostly flatters. "It's better to burn out than rust out," we say.

Saddled with work means we are ready to go and grow! And with "too much" we can always choose projects and causes to suit our mood or circumstances. *Busy is a good way out of the downer days.* Lesser or lighter loads leave us with too much time to whimper and whine. Obligation is good medicine! Ever noticed how those with the most work to do seem to weep and worry least? More people perish from boredom than from overload.

Successful people are busy. Busyness brings satisfying production, not unhappy wandering. It's accomplishment that truly satisfies! Successful people don't mind getting tired because rest after labor feels good. They go to bed not to escape in sleep, but to become refreshed so they can get up and go at it again. They wake in the morning expectant and enthusiastic. Besides, how can one rest from being idle?

Time whiners constantly complain about how busy they are... How little time they have to do the necessary. Very few successful people complain about time because neither the clock nor the calendar is very forgiving and what is lost is lost forever. It's just a fact that in our journey through daily demands, we are dropped in the battlefields of decisions competing for the use of our time. In other words, reading the newspaper, grocery shopping, and servicing the car, duel with celebrating a birthday, reading a bedtime story, and flossing teeth.

> *"What would be the use of immortality to a person who cannot use well half an hour?"*
> *—Ralph Waldo Emerson*

BEHIND IS A TIME ISSUE.

Being behind and late is *not* a life-style most of us want, and it's definitely not the life-style of the successful. We impose an urgency about others being on time—but not ourselves. We want the movie to start on time, checks to arrive when promised and meals ready to eat when we're hungry. But, we cry for flexibility when we pay bills and taxes, turn in the report, or start the meeting.

BEING BEHIND CAUSES,
- *Mistrust*
- *Misunderstandings*
- *Stress and worry*
- *Illness*
- *Accidents, even death*
- *Unemployment*
- *Poverty*
- *Loss of opportunity*
- *Loss of love*
- *Depression and guilt*
- *Further procrastination*
- *Late fees and overpayments*
- *Anger, rebellion, divorce*
- *Things to break and malfunction*
- *Damage to our self-esteem*
- *Impatience*
- *Mental agony*

Successful people manage their use of time—a secret they learn early. They are able to regulate the traffic in their lives and don't find themselves constantly behind. Behind is the sneaky first cousin of lazy and the sire of procrastination. It makes us late, reduces our opportunities to help others, and shatters confidence. Paying late, arriving late, RSVPing late, showing affection late, sleeping late, letting the dog out late, gassing the car late…everything on the late side of life has a trouble-making guarantee written all over it.

LATE SPEAKS CLEARLY AND IT SAYS,
- *I'm not really interested*
- *I'm inconsiderate*
- *I'm not ready*

Feeling behind in anything bothers most people. When we're behind in too many things, we're in toilet territory.

BEHIND-R-FLEX

- *I'm a little desperate*
- *I live for the moment*
- *I didn't plan*
- *I'm self-consumed*

According to time expert, Eileen Carlston, Ed.D, "Being late is a sign that the person has unresolved control issues." Requiring people to "wait" for us because we are running behind is a gross imposition.

Those who have to wait might be tolerant, even polite about it, but they don't like it a bit.

We say…
"I had a bad cell phone, couldn't check in."
"The power went off, so my alarm didn't work."
"There was this traffic jam…"
"I got this last-minute phone call…"

When we haven't got the job done, the assignment in, the item fixed, the habit broken, we're on the defense. On the ball field and in life, we don't score anything on defense. Successful teams are the ones with the ball, not the ones struggling to get it.

Feeling behind in anything bothers most people. When we're behind in too many things, we're in toilet territory.

Probably half of our anxiety and dissatisfaction with life is due to piled up, backed up "gonna do's," not anything we did wrong. You know, those pesky to–do's we haven't done, or promises we haven't kept. We've been carrying around those lists—like a chronic sore throat—forever. We're tending them, explaining them, going to sleep at night with them, reviewing them, and then waking up in the morning halfheartedly planning what to do with them. We reshuffle them, paw at them (wounding them a bit), and finally get a few out of our way!

Thank goodness for digital electronic organizers. At least now we don't have to rewrite our "To Do" list every new day—it's done automatically; but the entries aren't made on their own.

When there's too much "behind", we feel overwhelmed and buried alive. How many of these are you behind in?

CHECK OFF WHAT YOU'RE BEHIND IN...

❑ Payments
❑ Cleaning/Organizing
❑ Reading (that good book)
❑ Reading (magazines, newspapers, and business related articles)
❑ Filing
❑ Calling and writing friends and family
❑ Servicing vehicles
❑ Filing or paying taxes
❑ Weeding and planting
❑ Thank-you notes
❑ Saying "I love you"
❑ Making scrapbooks
❑ Personal medical checkup
❑ Immunizations
❑ Dental check up
❑ Appliance repairs

❑ Painting, carpeting, remodeling
❑ New Year's resolutions
❑ Exercise
❑ Prayer
❑ School/class assignments
❑ Organizing yourself and your surroundings
❑ Mailing in rebates
❑ Weight loss goal
❑ Social obligations
❑ Arriving at airports
❑ Taking care of personal hygiene
❑ Making decisions on important matters
❑ Taking necessary medications
❑ Answering e-mail, voice mail
❑ Will and Trust preparation
❑ Preparing for retirement

Procrastination is just a simple priority or a scheduling problem. We know what to do, but we just don't do it. *Behind* is a position that really limits our options. It's a sure way to prevent us from reaching peak performance, and ending up in toilet territory. Just about anything can become a time problem once we let it fall behind.

[SANDRA] *DeDe used the family car to get to and from college. Her dad's only request was that she maintain it. She knew it was time to get the oil changed but was too busy with work and classes to fit it into her schedule. Finally, the warning light started to come on but she still put it off, figuring the car would be okay a few more days. Driving on the freeway one day, the whole engine just froze up—no response when she pushed on the gas pedal. Three thousand dollars later, she had a new, replacement engine.*

If we don't get around to putting oil in the car, the engine is going to be ruined, even if we own an oil well and have fourteen funnels in the garage somewhere. Successful people know that they can't keep much of an eye open for the good ahead if they are dragging along, and tending, the burden of being behind.

STRATEGIES SUCCESSFUL PEOPLE USE TO AVOID BEING BEHIND THE LATE BALL: THEY,

- *Believe they own time; it doesn't own them*
- *Forget the idea that "there'll be more time later"*
- *Toss out the "I was born late" attitude—they know they have control over their schedules*
- *Make their path known. When they tell people where they are going, people will help or at least get out of the way*
- *Avoid other behinders*

SUCCESSFUL PEOPLE ARE SETTLERS.

The successful settle things—they don't keep carrying around a punishing load of *un-dones*. And they don't wait to change what is bothering them.

There is magic in making peace with ourselves. Usually, it's not the big battles but the little skirmishes we fight on multiple fronts that do us in. The satisfaction from the simple action of "settling" something is astounding. Our life quality hinges on the conclusions we reach and then turn into *actions*—not simply on the goals we mentally agree to (as so many books and seminars claim). Consider your life's dreams that are not becoming realities for you right now. The pathways to these dreams are unfinished. They hang there day after day, year after year.

Things on hold seldom help. All of the weight—financial, mental, physical, and spiritual—from the undone will remain with us like an unwelcome stepchild until it's settled. Without a day of closure, the carrying of undone things will continually punish us.

So often we judge ourselves "dumb" when in fact, it's simply "delay" that has blocked our progress. We have to return too often to deal with issues that we should have settled, but we waited and waffled instead.

Successful people face up to what they know bothers them. And they do this as many times as there are issues to untangle. They detest procrastination. They know that delay damages but dealing develops direction. Resolution returns them to real life—rescues them from treading toilet water. Settling is a timesaving virtue.

[DON] *Watching the construction of and paying for a new corporate building, I noticed how lack of settling a single simple issue multiplied into many costly problems. We were on a building schedule where one trade had to be coordinated with another trade as work progressed. The painting had to be done right after the sheetrock was up and perfa-taped, then we needed to install electrical fixtures, lay carpet, put furniture in place, and move in!*

The painter was ready, but the decorator couldn't decide on the color of the paint. They had two meetings, looked at the color chips, and held lengthy discussions but still no decision was made. With no color choice made, the painter was thrown off his schedule by a week. Others waited on the painter, but still no color from the decorator, so

If we trace most of our current problems, we'll find that they have as their catalyst something that wasn't settled somewhere up the line.

electrical and carpet workers had to move ahead, doubling the time and cost of painting when they finally settled on a color.

- *If a route on a trip is not settled before we go, the trip will cost more money and take more time.*
- *If where we are going to eat out isn't settled before we leave, we don't know what is proper to wear, so we can't get ready.*
- *If a little dispute or an IRS penalty or similar fine isn't settled now—it will double or triple later.*
- *If ill feelings between friends aren't settled, they won't be friends for long.*
- *If we can't settle on a time and place for the physical examination, we cannot get the test and diagnosis*

FREE TIME.

We scheme, serve, save, and sacrifice to have our free time. Yet when it comes, few of us handle it well. Free time seems to encourage carelessness and dilute discipline as marriages fail, spirituality lessens, health deteriorates, charity diminishes and enthusiasm fades. Nobleness seems to quickly decay in people who are not responsible in the use of their free time.

In the great menu of life, free time should be portioned out as a seasoning, not a serving, or worse yet, consumed as if it were an entire meal. Free time sprinkled here and there adds flavor and savor to the main menu. But to dream

of, live and eat for the salt, without the garden tomato to sprinkle it on, proves fatal to the human system.

Back in one of our college classes, we did something that was worth the whole semester. We analyzed the word "recreation," and discovered that it means to re-create feeling and energy. Well-designed recreation has positive healing value, and almost everyone benefits from it.

The professor pointed out, however, that once recreation is *expected* and scheduled, it loses some of its refreshing value.

WHAT IS GAINED FROM ENTERTAINED?

When we seek a change from our routines, what is the goal? Does the entertainment we tumble into meet our needs? We seek, hear, see, and breathe it so that gradually, we've slipped into a time toilet trap without realizing it. We involve ourselves for two weeks in pre-Super Bowl hysteria; we are willing to stand in long movie lines for new releases. And to what extremes do we go to win the lotteries for concerts?

Working out excessively at the gym, aimlessly wandering around the malls, constant golfing, hunting, happy hours, or frequenting the ski slopes all suck up time. They can become glamorous substitutes for being productive.

Even at home we are conditioned to share our eating space with music, television, or reading material. We can't hold a meeting, convention, or seminar without including some extravagant entertainment, the planning for which often exceeds the cost and effort invested in the reason for which we're meeting!

TV IS TOPS, ACCORDING TO POLL
What is your favorite way to spend an evening?

1. Watching television	31%
2. Being with family, husband, wife	20%
3. Reading	18%
4. Dining out	15%
5. Going to movies or theater	11%
6. Resting or relaxing	10%
7. Watching movies at home	7%
8. Visiting friends or relatives	6%
9. Entertaining friends or relatives	5%
10. Listening to music	4%

Total adds to more than 100 due to multiple responses —Gallup Poll

Consider the average club, school, or political meeting. We serve punch and cookies, and struggle to get some singers, jugglers, magicians or dancing girls to show up. We expect entertainment at the restaurants we frequent, too. The decorations, music, and mementos scream that entertainment is the real value—and they all take time.

THE "SHOW" ON THE ROAD.
We don't even take a trip without entertainment anymore. Once we listened to conversation as we traveled, or looked out the window at the panorama of the world. It was "Wow!" But now, we have movies and piped-in music on the airplane, and portable CD players to occupy us.

[DON] *On a recent family trip to California, I rode from the beach back to the hotel with six grandchildren, ages six through thirteen.*
There was ZERO social interaction. What we did have was a nice cartoon playing on the TV and two kids engrossed with laptop video computer games. The six-speaker stereo system in the Suburban was on full force. Two other kids had nice headsets with plush earphones. Spoiled? Probably. Just like everybody else riding on the entertainment treadmill.

Being "plugged in" equates to being "tuned out" of healthy social interaction.

GETTING AWAY FROM IT ALL?
Our push to get away to play is almost as prevalent as our over-the-counter drugging of ourselves. Travel and tourism rank as the third largest industry in the U.S., only behind health and business services.

Successful people make vacations and time off healthy and fun, but they don't expect a problem to disappear when they do. They know getting out of our daily routine from time to time can create a fresh, objective approach. On vacation doesn't necessarily mean away from impending obligation—in fact, it can delay or distract us from the process of eliminating our problems. Successful people know that they will return to water-treading territory after every escape; problems must ultimately be settled in their own environment. Vacation and time away *can* be valuable for stimulating fresh thoughts and insights to help solve these problems.

> *"I knew I'd traveled too much when the airlines offered to send me anywhere for a paid vacation, and I couldn't think of a single place I wanted to see."*

WATCHING THE ACTION.

Somehow we spend an inordinate amount of time *watching* what's going on, whether it's movies, live entertainers, or sports heroes. One successful friend made this bold decision on sports, "I don't want to waste time and emotion watching overpaid, arrogant athletes struggle on a big lawn." Somehow we don't feel quite as guilty about spending time on sports or hobbies when we participate vicariously.

Some of us are physically challenged because of age, injury or incident, however we can still make active use of our time and resources—no one has to be solely a bystander and succumb to perpetual TV watching, or spectating.

One of the big all-time sources of inactivity is TV.

[SANDRA] *After moving into our California home a few years ago, we planned to hook up to cable. We could get one clear news channel with our built-in antenna, but that was about all.*

Because it was February, we decided to wait until school was out before presenting the multi-channel temptations to our seven children living at home. June came and nobody seemed to be begging for TV. Soon we were busy with summer activities and thought, "wait until fall." The seasons came and left for three years before we gave into the tube. I still reminisce about those quieter days when we took the time to talk more easily and the children did their homework and perused the newspaper more thoroughly.

The average American spends thirteen years of his or her precious time on earth watching TV! Successful people aren't willing to let a good-sized piece of their life be sucked away by the tube.

> *Extra time will appear when we hit that new channel OFF once in awhile.*

The successful know that entertained is a dangerous substitute for maintained. Their world is not centered on entertainment and they don't use it like a religion to guide them. They don't bandage their blahs with a bombardment of comedy, sports contests, games, escapist movies, and blasting songs. Successful people don't place work and play at opposite ends of the spectrum of life—they learn to blend the two.

No matter how much fun is available, they refuse to get pulled into the bowl. *They don't party their lives into the potty.*

The "take it easy and enjoy yourself" reward that is forever being dangled before us today, is based on the premise of idleness—the chance to do nothing, not even projects you want to do. *People don't become successful because of time off.* Idleness gets old fast and cripples the mind, body and spirit. The old adage "an idle mind is the devil's workshop" proves pretty accurate. Lives are more often in the toilet when we are idle than when we keep ourselves busy.

ACCOMPLISHMENT: THE BEST RECREATION!

People who label others "workaholics" might be surprised to know that it's not just the love of their job that leads them to work long hours or weekends—it's the joy of the results and accomplishment from how they choose to use their time. This is the very reward others are desperately hunting for when they

escape to the tennis court, golf course, fishing stream or bar. Productive use of time serves the best menu in town for deep satisfaction.

Almost everyone we meet is struggling deep down, trying to be big in something—to be recognized and rewarded for accomplishment. What do we want to become an expert in—card shuffling? Wine tasting? Tidily winks? Game shows? Successful people want to be experts in something constructive that contributes. UFO watching, for

Vacations don't always end up like we expect.

example, might be great seasoning, but it's probably not much of a main course in life.

If we were to challenge a thousand of the smartest people around to come up with a list of things we might do to achieve a happy and toilet-free life— What secret or source of self-satisfaction would we find repeating itself on the list? I bet we would see one all-encompassing action that could out-perform all the others.

SERVICE: THE ULTIMATE USE OF TIME

We need to feel we've made a difference in someone else's life to feel good about our own. Service means spending some time giving of self to build and encourage, or restore life and hope to someone else. Service doesn't make us servants. Service to others makes us a master in control of our means and abilities. There's an inherent good in wanting to serve.

[DON] *The many modern-day free spirits (hippies) living easy life-styles on the island Kauai, Hawaii have always intrigued me. One day, I said to my wife, "What is it about these people? They're nice and polite and they don't bother anyone. On the other hand, they don't do much for anyone else. They seldom contact their families or join in community service. They seem to have a sort of distant spirit about them."*

"It's the spirit of self-absorption," she said.

Generally speaking, those who are most unhappy are obsessed with themselves. They complain because they only have the needs of one person on their mind.

Most unsuccessful folks treasure up time and assets totally for them. "Mine" is the word they live by, but attractive as that may seem, hoarding assets of money, love, talent and especially time seldom brings happiness.

We all know people who refuse to do anything for the community, the church, the parks, the poor, the young, the old, or even *their* relatives. They may be decent people in general, but their weekends are their weekends, for their fun and their benefit entirely. It's amazing how much of what we read today is solidly rooted in narcissism—or spending time on one's self. That's the worst advice anybody could give for lasting satisfaction.

Thank goodness there are plenty of successful people out there who do share their time and personal resources with others. More people than ever are serving, helping and making a difference. They carve out many hours a week for Little League, 4-H, school, scouts, needy neighbors, the church, the environment, the aged, service groups, libraries, foster kids, and so forth. They gain immense pleasure from sharing their love, cars, home, money, talents, food, and time.

We are subject to laws of natural selection and must sometimes make difficult decisions about our decision to serve. For example, "Do I lecture to nine hundred women and offer some needed inspiration or do I stay at home and participate in a private family birthday party?" The best choice isn't always the easy choice. Should immediate family always have priority for our time? Is it always better to pass on our inheritance of money (which represents time) to family members, or to a charity or other worthy cause? When a doctor takes fifteen years to prepare for his profession, does that justify his sacrifice and trade-off of family time during those years of medical school training? And what about the time he devotes to others once he's in full-time practice, especially if he is not remunerated?

[SANDRA] *A young ophthalmologist barely out of residency training spent his entire Thanksgiving week holiday in Central America. He was invited to accompany doctors who (as they'd been doing for years now) gave service without fee to the poor in isolated, under-served towns. Numerous operations were performed to restore sight and stop disease in those who would otherwise be unable to get medical assistance. The doctor was energized and fulfilled as he brought health and sight to many of the locals.*

Nine of the fourteen children between our two families have served

volunteer church missions, so far. This 18-24 month commitment involves not only proselytizing, but humanitarian service. These young ones from the ages of nineteen to twenty-three choose for a period of time to set aside their personal desires (schooling, marriage, vocations) and give extra time to serving others. They leave all loved ones behind, and exist at their own expense on bare necessities in their new cultural surroundings.

Service is an effective serum for any malady.

Our immediate sons and daughters have served in Asia, South America, Central America, Canada, Eastern Europe, the Caribbean, and throughout the U.S. They've done things such as gather up debris and bury dead animals after Hurricane Gilbert in Jamaica, clean out bedpans in old folks' homes in neglected towns in Ukraine, paint government monuments on St. Kitts, build starter homes in Brazil, teach English classes in Romania and serve the deaf in the cities of Baltimore and New York.

But we do not need to leave home to be an emissary for good. Giving freely of our time in any place or way develops character.

Successful people take a firm stand on how they will use their time, and are stimulated by spending it on teams, with families, staffs, and organizations dedicated to good causes.

> *Most people say they volunteer because they are needed or feel a duty to help. Studies show that the more hours we work, the more we volunteer.*

Service is an effective serum for any malady. Doing something worthwhile for others performs the simple magic of making us forget ourselves, and when we change that focus, our problems fade. It's difficult to be self-occupied when we have a cause greater than ourselves, and we're working to help others out of their predicaments.

A family had been taking care of their aging mother, waiting on her and filling her various needs. It was a big part of their lives and they were glad to be able to help her. But gradually the mother became weaker and weaker, mentally and physically. She began losing her will to live and was sinking fast. The family checked her into a hospice facility, where she was lovingly tucked into a two-bed patient room, most likely for the last time.

In bed #2 next to their mother was an even older woman in very poor condition, whose days were also obviously numbered. She was far from her family and scarcely able to feed herself.

Seeing some neglect by hospice workers, the mother made an immense effort to get out of her own bed and shuffle over to the weeping woman. She began comforting her by rubbing her feet, and helping her get to a drink. The older woman responded with an immediate smile.

Next morning, after an orderly had mechanically performed the basic survival duties for the older woman in bed #2, the mother again got out of bed and cleaned her up a bit more. She also combed the woman's hair, showed her some pictures, and sat at her side for more than an hour. That evening, the mother again came to her side and read to her until she dozed off. The more the mother helped, the less the staff did for both of them, and the more they praised their independence. Within weeks, instead of shuffling, the mother scrambled to help and pamper her roommate. An enthusiastic smile and new strength came to the older woman as well as to the mother. Within two weeks the children checked their mother out of the hospice, seemingly fifteen years younger than when she was admitted.

The mother lived several more independent, productive years—without pills, formal therapy, or wheelchairs. The only prescription necessary was simple, no cost, enjoyable *service*.

A DOZEN MORE WAYS SUCCESSFUL PEOPLE – CONTROL THEIR CLOCK AND CALENDAR

1. *Toil when tired, walk while wounded, hustle while hurting*
2. *Don't pursue piddly paths*
3. *Travel light*
4. *Be multi-faceted; piggyback*
5. *Take little time for politics or the petty*
6. *Don't get into self-pity*
7. *Don't worship dining*
8. *Know when to fix and when to forget*
9. *Take time to serve and volunteer*
10. *Anticipate and prepare*
11. *Don't shop much*
12. *Don't indulge in selfish rituals*

Doing for others ends up being the most personally benefiting thing we can do, and certainly one of the best ways successful people can use their time.

Doing for others ends up being the most personally benefiting thing we can do, and certainly one of the best ways successful people can use their time.

"I don't know what your destiny will be, but one thing I know is— the only ones among you who will be happy are those who have sought and found how to serve..."
—Albert Schweitzer

CHAPTER 5

"My parents fed me too much as a child."

"Super Size it!"

"How about dessert?"

"Got seconds?"

"They should make fast foods more nutritious."

"I just can't get going in the morning without that second cup of coffee."

"Other people have higher metabolisms."

"That Ab-Exerciser was just a piece of junk."

Bodies Are Not Burdens to Successful People

From about eight years old and up we worry about and work on having the perfect body—first for vanity, later for endurance and finally for plain survival. We are flogged with a constant media campaign of ideals, medicines, machines and makeovers to keep us young, attractive and energetic. Advertisements and store displays are dominated by pills and plans which promise an outcome of living longer, feeling better, and attaining a body that is lean and sexy. We may have different ideas for the best route to beauty or vitality, but one thing for sure, *EVERYONE AGREES BAD HEALTH IS A BUMMER.*

Yet, most of us make unrealistic demands on our bodies. No matter what we pour in them or put on them, they are extremely forgiving. They digest, absorb, adapt, recover, and come through year after year! Overall, if we want success, we need to have the strongest, most willing body possible.

SUCCESSFUL PEOPLE DON'T SPEND MUCH TIME SICK OR AILING.

We must first recognize that lots of good, talented, productive people are challenged with bodies that compromise their capabilities, due to previous injury, illness, birth defects, genetics, age and so on. This group did not self-induce limitations on their bodies. They are restricted or handicapped by circumstances beyond their control.

The rest of us have little excuse for allowing our bodies not to function optimally. Any excess in, on, or around a body is a burden, period. We are reminded fifty times a day what is good or not good for us. At the extreme, we are haunted by visions of vigorous men and women models in swimsuits, sweating on deluxe exercisers.

HEALTH ON THE JOB.

Feeling good and job success are in partnership today more than ever, as employee well-being and health maintenance costs to employers become prime considerations in hiring. If we show up for a job interview with a degree, talent, experience and good references but are in poor physical condition, our chance to secure the job is less likely. Bad health habits are a red flag to a company's health and life insurance programs. No employer wants to foot the bill for unhealthy staff. It may be unfair (the way we look upon and treat those who are out of condition), but it's a reality.

A human resources committee interviewed a job candidate, and as one of the members put it later, "He didn't have a chance when he walked into the meeting—panting for breath, munching mints and straining his shirt buttons, to say nothing of his bloated red nose. All of this was topped off by a sweaty-palm hand shake."

Many of us set our life expectancy gauge as if we don't need to worry about living past age sixteen, by the way we eat, drink, and drug ourselves into premature old age. It is odd that we spend so much time and money on cosmetics, machines, and clothes to make ourselves beautiful and trim, but adopt risky living habits that make us ugly. Over baked-in-the-sun skin, nicotine stained teeth and bloating bellies all result from bad health choices. To stay healthy in a day of unhealthy options is not easy. We spend much more time and money to decorate the body than we do to deliver it from the perils of deterioration. In fact, Americans spend more on maintaining their cars than on maintaining their bodies!

[DON] *I was just six years old, but not too young to be impressed by the appraisal made by my Uncle Shay. It was a beautiful fall morning and we stepped outside preparing for a family pheasant hunt. Uncle Shay beat his chest, looked into the sky, and said, "You know Donny, the sun looks better coming up at 60 than it ever has!" While I remember this vividly, I didn't comprehend the full meaning. By the time I was 60 myself, I understood it perfectly—feeling good and having good health is nearly everything. It is more valuable than having fame, property or position.*

We can do and be anything as long as our health holds out. Many people, who are not able to be healthy by choice or chance, state it very well: "You are so lucky to be healthy!" One goal of success is not only to be healthy as we grow, but also to be healthy when we are old.

That's a big victory! And it places us far out of the toilet!

GIMMIE, GIMMIE.

Everyone believes in good health. Convincing is no problem. It's the *conduct* to get there that we all struggle with. It is so easy and so natural to give the body what it wants whenever it wants—and it generally feels great doing it. Consequences (like constipation) usually are a delayed punishment. Taste is so *now* and cholesterol so *later* that we almost begin to live with a "who cares" attitude—really a slow bankruptcy of our bodies. More than half of us eat too much, and these extra pounds cost the average overweight person $5,000 in added health-care bills over a lifetime, according to a study published in the American Journal of Preventive Medicine. And let's not overlook the $33 billion we spend annually on weight-loss products and services to get rid of the ingested delights that accumulate so innocently on our bellies and thighs.

THE QUESTION OF QUEEN SIZE

If you've wondered about the guys,
What it is that gets their eyes,
Wherein for them attraction lies,
What will make their temperature rise—

Here's a truth to make you wise.
Never let yourself matronize.
Very few men like oversize,
A body plumped with good French fries.

Men like to watch a female glide,
Without shaking a big backside,
Women who in health take pride,
Who don't wear clothes that lap and hide.

They like you to remain a bride,
To find a waist where a belt is tied.
So keep your honey satisfied,
Avoid the curse of getting wide.

THE QUESTION OF KING SIZE

If you've wondered about the gals,
What men we want to be our pals,
Why we primp and take great care
With how we walk and what we wear—

We don't mind bald but here's the rut…
When you gorge you get a gut.
And then you plop—it drives us crazy,
We hate soft men, and detest lazy.

Get off your duff! Put down the paper.
We want a body with a taper.
Pump the iron, jog the path,
We'll then share love, instead of wrath.

But here you lounge—our sofa's shot,
A new divan I finally bought.
You'll not move? You're there to stay?
Then, "It's a set…take them both away!"

Weight gain is a problem for most of us. We just read the results of a study of 2500+ church-going people who made a self-assessment of their size. These are folks who live strict dietary guidelines that include no caffeine, smoking or alcohol. Yet 73 percent of the group considered themselves overweight.

By 150 calories a day, our portions are bigger than twenty years ago. This alone adds up to an extra 15 pounds a year (Don't we all know that!). Ironically, we still justify super-sizing our double cheeseburger and order of fries by tagging on a *diet* drink.

Pain is seldom weighted objectively if it is spaced far enough from the pleasure that preceded it. That's why it seems almost an injustice when some "hogs" consume pastries in quantity and sparkle skinny, while the rest of us merely read a milk shake ad and seem to gain two pounds. Weight is not the sole indicator of health, however.

[DON] *For a time I was a spokesperson for one of America's major manufacturers. Now it looks easy to get big pay to stand in a classy booth in a new suit—visit, shake hands, and do short demos. Wrong, man! It's murder—twice as hard as pick and shovel labor. By the end of the day—back, legs, mind, and body are gone.*

By 6 PM. (having started at 7 am) I could barely stagger through the lobby and collapse in my room. I ordered in a salad, wrote, watched a little AMC, and went to bed by 10 o'clock.

But my colleagues were apparent men of iron. They worked a grueling schedule along side me (sneaking off only for frequent smokes), and at the end of the day enthusiastically figured out where the best Chicago eating places were. After dinner they would drink until 11 PM, socialize around the bars until midnight, and then chase women. About the time I was ready to get up, I'd hear them rioting down the hall to their rooms. A few hours later, the blurry-eyed partying bunch would feel their way into the breakfast room, grab a large cup of coffee and several plastic-glazed donuts, and be ready for action. The next day it was the same drill, and the next just the same.

Later, during a rigorous treadmill running test at my annual physical, I asked my doctor about these guys. "How could this be? Are lots of coffee, booze and glazed donuts super foods for some people? How can you function on a diet like that and three hours sleep a night?"

The doctor chuckled and said, "Those guys are like knights on a mighty horse, brandishing a gleaming sword, galloping and lapping up all their wine, women, and song. At age 45-50 they will fall off the horse and spend their remaining years fighting health problems—slaves to seriously restricted diets and limited activities."

That response was a fair appraisal on the apparent injustice of overindulgence. Many over-fed, over-pleasured people *claim* to still feel healthy because they preserve their bodies by embalming them prematurely. Our goal ought to be to *die young* as *late* as possible.

The miracle of the media doesn't help responsible healthy living. They promote intake without bellyache. Advertisers want us to feel good *this* weekend and forget about next week's consequence. The unspoken attitude we absorb here is that it's OK to eat and drink *however* much, *whenever* we're inclined, and *whatever* is offered, without effect.

Government agencies add to the problem as well. For example, is everything that is approved by the USDA and served in a clean A-rated restaurant necessarily good for us? No! We still have the final say on food choices and amounts.

We really can't blame the mirror or the scale for what we see after years of overfeeding ourselves. "Is there something or someone out there, that caused this grotesque buildup on my body?" we cry. Nope. It's all our own doing.

On a plane from St. Louis, a passenger was returning home after months of being away on a big construction project. His entire banner-waving family greeted him. After the usual hugs and kisses they headed for the baggage area. As the wife attempted to put her arm around her husband, she said gently, "Honey, you're a little larger than you were."

The man launched into a tirade. "Yes, those sons of guns! *! just fed us to death! You wouldn't believe how much food and drink they served."

Had they really pried his mouth open and shoveled it in? Apparently. It was "their" fault entirely; those jerks who set out the Ding Dongs, served up the cheesecake, glazed the donuts and fried the potatoes.

There are signs on some restaurants that read, "All You Can Eat!" Is this much different than saying, "Welcome to the Hog Trough"? We could probably eat until we drop over dead. The confusion between all we *can* eat and all we *should* eat is apparent in the recent rise in overweight numbers. Successful people know there is no bargain in bloating, and no salvation for the body or mind in suffering. Bigger portions only yield bigger delayed punishment.

Some airlines serve snacks or munchies on each flight, especially if it's more than two hours. Before and after each meal almost everyone aboard will order a drink as offered; it's like an obligation. How do the airlines know how much our body should absorb while flying? More importantly, why do we feel it is necessary to eat or drink all that is offered? For some reason, whether we are in the air or on the ground, functions call for food.

[SANDRA] *I once headed a committee that went to great lengths to organize an inspiring conference for women in the community. It was a well-publicized annual event, featuring popular speakers. I expected at least 200 attendees, but was disappointed when only 70 women showed up. The only thing I'd done differently from previous years was to eliminate the light meal at the conclusion of the evening.*

The following year we held the function again, but announced in bold letters that a light supper would be served. More than 250 women attended this time.

Climbing the ladder of success might include passing up some nibbles along the way, because sometimes it's more important to feed our souls than our bodies.

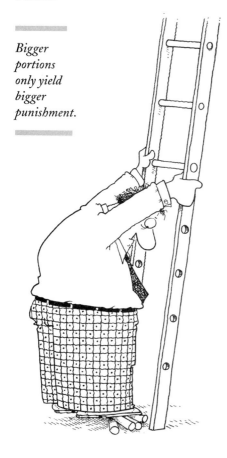

Bigger portions only yield bigger punishment.

HYPOCHONDRIAC HEIST.

Many people get lost in a forest of details about minor health ailments that really don't matter. They are possessed with going to the doctor or chatting with friends about what is wrong with them and others they know. They are into long lists of guessing and predicting games, instead of just eating well for optimum health. Their focus is on pills to fix problems. From Cigna Tel-Drug Program we learn that 60% of all prescription medications are "maintenance medications." These include drugs for high blood pressure, diabetes, cholesterol lowering medications, and so on. In time, many of us require more pills to fix the problems our first pills create as our dependence escalates. It is not surprising that since 1972, the number of drug prescriptions dispensed from retail outlets and through mail order has risen more than 50 percent— while our population has only increased 8% in the same period!

There are many options or ways people keep records of their day-to-day life. Some do it by keeping a journal, others do it by tape-recorder, many with the idea they will one day write an autobiography.

[SANDRA] *One woman I knew had so many empty prescription bottles, she could use them for a complete earth-life historical reference. I found them, stashed by the hundreds, as I helped dejunk her old stuff one spring day. They dated back to 30 years ago, each brown bottle bearing the name of the drug, ailment it was to treat, date, and dose amount. A perfect reference system!*

Drugs tend to become a big thing for us, especially as we get older. They are a security, a pet and protection of some type. We gloat about the numbers of them we ingest each day. Where once we had a fairly inconspicuous pillbox of some style, we now have inlaid, automatic dispensing machines as big and functional as an ergonomic computer keyboard that dole out our dosages for the month and beyond.

Successful people insulate themselves from many ugly outcomes by monitoring their medicines. They don't use drugs for relief from reality. They shun uppers and downers and other pills that artificially stimulate what the body is meant to do on its own, if it is able.

IT'S A RAT RACE

[DON] *Years ago, in my college health class, we reviewed an experiment I'll never forget. Miniature baby bottles with feeding nipples were put around the interior of a big cage. The bottles were either filled with an unhealthy sugary fluid or life-sustaining, healthy juices.*

Hungry rats were then turned loose and left alone for several days in this small animal food court. All of the rats sniffed and sampled the palate-pleasing bottles of sweet, sugary fluid. They feasted on them until they were sick and staggering around as only sugar-high rats can do.

It turns out the rats weren't so dumb after all. After three days of gluttony, they finally figured out what was making them feel bad and gradually swung their diets over to the healthy juices. They became robust-looking, lively, and vigorous.

Successful people eat well but they don't center their lives on food. With time, healthy food choices become second nature. Like our smart rats, they can figure out for themselves, which diets are sensible and which make them sluggish.

Often we see educated, intelligent humans, even some physicians and nutrition experts, who defiantly make bad food, drug, and drink choices. They stay addicted to them year after year, even though they know it may eventually do them in.

"Eat well 80 percent of the time and go ahead and blow it 20 percent of the time so you don't feel deprived," say some fitness gurus. But intentionally "blowing it" is not a widespread trademark of the successful. Unwise consumption is a ricocheting bullet. Few dodge it well, but successful people never step on the firing range.

[SANDRA] *During one of my graduate courses in nutrition, my instructor said, "If you are selective enough in what you eat, you probably won't need to take daily vitamins. If you do take them, it's like flushing 50 cents down the toilet each day.*

Why is this so, I wondered? She then explained that popping a vitamin pill or two might take care of the most critical nutritional requirements—but vitamin pills are meant to be a supplement. They are not meant to substitute for foods that naturally provide and enhance. If we eat right, we will ingest all the nutrients we need. She further cautioned that we should eat sensible amounts and choose foods that don't harm our bodies.

"Don't kill your body off with bad food choices before you are ready to be buried," she taught.

In other words, there are no magic pills or shortcuts around eating well. Supplements should not be substitutes for a healthful diet. We can't just scarf up unhealthy foods and make up the difference by taking vitamins. Food choices alone can tack as many as 13 years onto a person's de facto age—or strip off as many as 14, according to Ann Underwood, nutrition research writer. It's still crystal clear that the healthiest regimens are based on fruits, vegetables, whole grains, fish, nuts, low-fat dairy and small amounts of lean meat. Successful people gobble the "greens" and the "grains."

During a TV interview with then aging singing cowboy, Gene Autry, there was some comment about his growing older. He quipped, "Well, if I'd known I was going to live this long, I'd have taken better care of this body."

Actually, Autry did have a healthy mind and body. He worked hard physi-cally, avoided the easy life of too much food and drink, and relished mental challenges. He was a respected singer, actor, and successful businessman. He used it, and didn't lose it, living happily to age 91.

People have been galvanized to re-evaluate the complexity of their lives, particularly since the early 90's. After all the books, charts, talks and studies have concluded and been published, the bottom line tells us to use wisdom in eating and in our daily living habits.

Don't kid yourself, successful people have the same temptations and struggles with eating, drinking, and drugs as everyone else. Their victory comes in self-control and avoidance of the extremes. They aren't more intelligent or noble, but they do usually manage to look beyond the moment to see the likely consequences. Simple, but it works for them.

Options are wonderful in what to eat and what to drink, as in anything. The challenge here is that the thousands of options in our affluent society call for just as many careful judgments to be made. Most of us know what is good and not good for us, but even the smartest of us can be "first with the worst," seeking immediate pleasure and ignoring the potential for distress and pain later. Successful people ingest the best and leave the rest.

[DON] *Eating in a fancy New York restaurant not long ago, I had some kind of tasteless fish, embalmed in a highly spiced batter about two inches thick. My dinner partner said, "This is probably deep fried Kleenex." I agreed. You could have rolled a tissue up and dipped and fried it and few would have realized the difference.*

The United States is prosperous, but on the whole we have a sedentary lifestyle. In fact, we are the second fattest society on earth (first place goes to a tribe in the South Pacific).

WE DON'T BECOME WHAT WE DON'T EAT!

Drugs don't rule the lives of the successful because they are not dependent on repeated rounds of artificially induced pleasure. Shakespeare summed it up well, "O fools that put things in their mouths to steal away their brain."

When the administrator of a state mental hospital was asked what the most common cause of patient's confinement, she said, "Ninety percent are here because of alcohol or drug-related problems."

George Will of the *Washington Post* said that America's hideously costly health-care crisis is aggravated by unwise behavior,

"At least $1 out of every $4 Americans spend on health care each year goes to treat conditions that have resulted from alcohol abuse, drug use, smoking, overeating, and other potentially changeable behaviors."

Not only does unwise consumption provoke our health care crisis—it can easily land us deep in toilet water. Successful people don't adopt behaviors that later force them to spend time and money in recovery programs.

WHAT'S MY WEAKNESS?

The drug speedometer or odometer may not be mounted on our forehead, but it's there inside, putting miles on us. Just about everyone in our civilized society uses drugs, the only question is what kind, and to what degree.

Today, bookstores have not just shelves, but whole sections devoted to recovery from addiction—then there are several more sections of novels that through subtle plots feed ideas to readers on how to *get* addicted! It's not just by accident that we get hooked on bad stuff.

If we can't go at least a day without our drugs (tobacco, alcohol, coffee), fat-laden burger, fries, pastries, N & N's, Big Swig, or whatever unhealthy thing our body craves, we could be mentally or physically addicted. *Successful people are not addicted; they leave the harmful stuff alone.*

Cocaine, heroin and other hard drugs

Alcohol, Tobacco

Caffeine (coffee, colas, chocolate)

Sleeping pills, Pain killers

How fast are we traveling and how far have we gone?

I'M NOT BLOWING SMOKE.

In our war on drugs, the simple value of living to feel and "look good for a lifetime" is seldom sold to us. We only get the negatives such as punishments for breaking the law, the chance of early death, relationships that will be ruined and so on. Successful people rally to the banner of the healthy edge that gives keenness and love and worth to living. Drugs of any kind, mild or strong, blunt that edge. This alone is reason enough to shun them ALL… totally, except where necessarily prescribed by a physician.

Cigarette smoking deserves some additional mention because it is still a big player on the drug scene and is well worth avoiding for reasons besides lung cancer and emphysema.

HE KICKED BUTT.

Walter Bowman wasn't just the leading statesman in his Idaho community; he was one of the most successful farmers around. And he was about the nicest man you'd ever hope to know… rough and tough, yet kind. Everybody looked up to him and listened when he spoke because he didn't speak often. But when he did, it was worth listening to. Walter shares his story.

I started smoking like lots of young ranch cowboys when I was fifteen or sixteen, so by age thirty I was pretty well addicted. When I found out all the deadly facts about cigarettes, and knowing I had two young sons, I decided to quit.

So I threw all my remaining cartons in the fire and went for it. I'm usually smart and strong enough to stick with something when I've decided it's important, but for some reason I felt like a scuba diver with no air in my tanks. I guess old habits involve not only mental and emotional addiction, but physical, too.

Finally, after weeks of agony, I felt I was gaining ground—truly on my way to kicking the habit. When I felt weak, I'd take long rides on my horse into the desert, away from any source of tobacco smell or temptation. On one of those crisp Idaho mornings, when fall was in the air and when a cigarette would taste best, came my test. I found myself miles into the desert. There were no roads, and surely only the Indians had trod there.

I was following a little trail and suddenly the horse stopped. There, as if artfully arranged by a New York ad agency, lay a beautiful, new, full pack of my favorite brand of cigarettes right there on the ground.

"Surely a mirage", I thought. But it wasn't. It was a perfectly fresh pack of cigarettes calling to me. Who knows where they came from? Perhaps they spilled out of an earlier rider or hunter's pocket? Not even a demon would do this to a desperate man.

"No one would know... maybe just one?" I thought to myself.

Then I kicked my horse and rode over the pack. I took another route home so I wouldn't have to see that lusty camel blinking up at me.

And guess what? After that experience, I beat it... and never smoked again. I lost the desire entirely.

You might say that Walter Bowman cleared his habit like a "puff of smoke." We can all ride right over our unsuccessful behavior if we really desire it badly enough. While we may not know or be able to control precisely how healthy we are, we usually know whether or not we are creating additional risk factors for ourselves. And we don't have to wait for our personal wake-up call:

[SANDRA] *My friend was a good husband and devoted father of four. When he decided to get some additional life insurance the company required a standard chest x-ray. He was nervous about the exam because he'd been a moderate smoker for more than twenty years.*

The films were developed by the technician late in the day and wouldn't have a final reading by the radiologist until morning. But there it was, a small opaque spot in the lower right lung, visible even to the untrained eye.

David left the office stunned, dreading to share the news with his wife and family. He didn't sleep that night and prayed that somehow the x-rays were mistaken. He vowed to the Almighty he'd stop smoking and put his health back in order if he could have one more chance.

Next morning, the radiologist called. The spot was simply a small artifact (defect) on the x-ray film itself. His lungs were clear. David was jubilant, overcome with thankfulness. He'd been given a second chance with his "wake-up call" to break the deadly habit. But the jolting experience didn't last. Soon David was back at it.

His final turning point came some months later when his young daughter pleaded with her daddy to stop smoking. He was moved, and straight away enrolled in a smoking cessation program at the local university. The commitment kicked in and David is smoke-free to this day, some two years later.

Successful people act on their impulses to change a habit they don't like. If they need help to fight it, they aren't ashamed to ask for it.

ALCOHOL ADVERSITIES.

A wheelchair-bound young man was being interviewed for a book on how to make cleaning easier for the handicapped. He was a handsome fellow, only twenty-four-years old. On his table was a picture of his two precious daughters and a lovely wife.

Can I Fix You a Drink?

He recalled drinking it up with the boys one Saturday night and rolling his pickup. The result was permanent damage to his arms and legs as well as injury to his spirit. Because of his continued drinking *after* the accident, his wife and the girls moved out. The interviewer spied two garbage cans overflowing with fresh, empty, crushed beer cans in the corner.

His continued addiction first crippled his body, then his spirit, and finally cut other significant ties. A too typical prelude to an unsuccessful future—a toilet tragedy.

Society keeps searching for justifiable reasons for the use of alcohol in any amount. When we use it, to any degree, we are also endorsing its effect on mankind. It seems below the dignity of any successful man or woman to imbibe.

"*They* got me drunk," said the young man to the judge, after an unintentional homicide and unbelievable destruction of property. For successful people, there are no *theys* around, getting them into or out of problems.

IN MODERATION.

One Idaho county commissioner explained the drinking dilemma well in his satirical report on alcohol abuse as he reported,

"*Last year in one state, 10,000 people died from drinking-related problems, and one person from a dog bite. So they shot the dog and licensed the liquor.*"

Makes sense, huh? Our nation's approach to so many physically and emotionally damaging substances is often not to cut them out, but to ration and control them in some kind of social appeasement. Then we have to raise funds and increase the budget to handle administration of the programs, and the negative results of it all. That's got to be some of the dumbest thinking ever.

Our health is really basic to all else we have to work with. The successful don't hide behind the idea that potentially harmful things may be "okay in moderation," especially when it comes to ethics and the well being of the human mind and body. How can one do anything ultimately destructive in a moderate way? If it's bad, it's bad!

- *Do we want moderate crime in our neighborhood?*
- *Anybody mind being diagnosed with a moderate case of cancer?*
- *Do we want to chance being moderately poisoned?*
- *Will our mate be OK with the fact that we commit adultery in moderation?*
- *Do we want to be on the road with moderately drunk drivers?*
- *Is there such a thing as moderate murder?*

Another variation on this logic is, "Adults Only" beverages. In other words, when you're old enough to know better, then you are allowed drink. Sorry kids, you can't pollute and ruin your body with tobacco and booze because it is dumb, risky, and will kill you. Wait until you're eighteen and twenty-one respectively, then you can do it. Duh.

FITNESS AND MORE.

We have never seen such ingenious inventions and machines as those trying to recondition American bodies. Some of these contraptions, to the nonuser, appear more vicious than the torture machinery on display in old English castle dungeons.

Successful people who are blessed with whole bodies know that healthy living isn't an unattainable goal; it's a series of small daily choices. Whether you are a 26-year-old mother-to-be, or a 76-year-old retiree, to stay fit takes constant care.

[SANDRA] *I began daily walks early in 1996 because all medical reports seemed to promise it would increase a person's energy—something I started thinking about more seriously in my 50's. Walking meant I would need to get up an hour earlier in the morning and somehow that seemed in conflict with getting enough rest. Nevertheless, I decided to give it a try. So before the clock struck six, my husband and I started a new life and climbed out of bed to put in our three miles in the hills behind our home. In less than two months, what seemed like a huge effort to get up earlier was somehow gone. Early mornings became a time he and I actually looked forward to. We talked and laughed as we walked, and gained more vitality then we hoped for.*

Then in January of 2001, I started to skip these daily three-mile (45-min) walks that had become a five-year habit. I had lots of good excuses for letting my program wane—a bout with the flu, a lengthy trip, stay-over company (twice)… In just four months my scale read six pounds heavier. The reality of extra pounds jolted me back into my exercise pattern, and the weight started to come off once again.

Every hour spent in vigorous exercise as an adult is repaid with two hours of additional life span according to Jerry Adler, fitness writer for *Newsweek*. But making the decision to exercise is strictly our personal business. For some people, the case for exercise just hasn't appeared on their radar screen. That's probably why one in three Americans over age 50 is completely sedentary. The other two have made their commitment and are successfully involved in *some* kind of exercise for health. Still, only 15% of us exercise at least four times per week, one hour per session. Exercise is just about the hardest commitment we have to make in our adult life, but it pays off with big, big rewards. Along with food choices, it can add on or subtract more than a dozen *years* from our effective life span.

PREVENTIVE MEASURES.

Preventive health care is extremely misunderstood. It's not just about getting vaccinations and annual physicals—it also tells us, "Eat right and exercise responsibly so as to lower that cholesterol or sugar (or whatever) so it won't advance beyond the acceptable ranges." As mentioned earlier, to consume a prescription drug to *lower* levels of anything out-of-range just to stop *another* more serious problem from developing means we've already let the problem advance too far. It's like double-checking for a jack and spare tire in the car trunk, before driving through a load of dumped nails on the highway. *It's smarter to change our route than plan for the consequence.*

We are told to brush and floss our teeth, but in spite of our best efforts, occasionally a tooth (or whatever else on our body) needs repair. If handled in time, it might be fixed for $100. To restore it later might increase pain, extend repair time and push cost up to $500 or more. When inevitable health problems do appear, successful people get on top of them immediately.

There is also the matter of becoming aware of conditions we have or are prone to have which might be potentially serious. A medical acquaintance of ours who operates an ultrasound service and is in the business of detecting and confirming certain conditions, gave an alarming opinion. He estimates that around 80% of killer diseases could be cured by earlier detection. Most of the responsibility for initiating preventive tests at the recommended ages, along with following treatment guidelines from physicians and preventive health care specialists, rests on *our* shoulders.

More and more practitioners now stress preventing health problems before they arise. Reed Phillips, DC, Ph.D., says, "The body ultimately heals itself. We just need to make it easier, not harder, for this to happen. Short-term specific goals for getting healthy and fit should be stressed over long-term, less specific goals."

According to Pamela Peeke, MD, the "mind, mouth and muscle are all critical components" to health. Thus, responsible lifestyle choices, along with doable diet and nutrition strategies help successful people prevent illness, maintain good health, and slow or reverse the effects of chronic disease and aging.

If we are 15 years of age our chances of death are one in 2,000 per year. By age 50, one in 66 of us will succumb. And by 100 years of age, our chances of dying are 50% each year. Our bodies are designed to last only so long. But with preventive care and responsible maintenance, we'll be successful in living healthier—longer, while successfully meeting our life's goals.

CHAPTER 6

My spouse is a
spender."

Those darn credit
cards."

It's that stingy
company I work for…"

The lousy stock
market…"

Do you think money
grows on trees?"

The president has sure
messed up the
economy…"

Do I look like Daddy
Warbucks?"

My partner really
cheated me.""

Successful People are Masters of Money

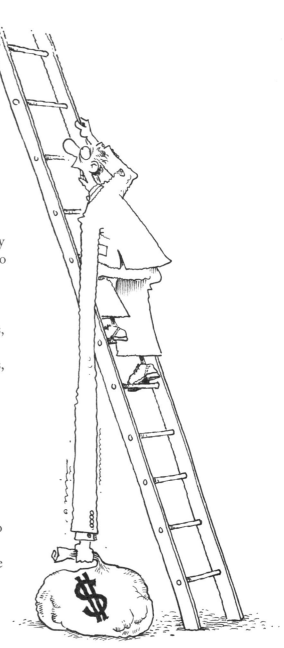

No one has perfect money wisdom, but successful people still don't struggle much with it. They have prepared themselves to earn it, and are willing to work for it. They have the ability to direct it to the right channels in their lives, which gives them great satisfaction. In other words, successful people handle money; they don't allow it to handle them.

CAN WE THINK RICH AND GROW RICH?

Think and grow rich is a wrong translation of the path to success. We hear so much hype from positive thinking crowds that all we have to do is "believe" to accomplish anything.

We could sit around and believe in being a piano virtuoso—but we will get there only by practicing and studying under a good teacher. We can watch golf on television for hours, but it isn't likely to reduce our handicap simply by seeing and believing we are a great player. Likewise, we have to *work* to be a winner with our money. Belief is important, but it's only a first step to success in the supervision of money.

[SANDRA] *Ken and Janice were typical folks who had a small but nice home, and three great kids. Ken had a good paying full-time job and Janice took care of incidental expenses with her part-time employment.*

When they had a chance to move to a bigger home in a nicer neighborhood, it seemed like the right thing to do, especially when they qualified so easily for the bigger loan. The larger monthly house payments began to suck up money that formerly paid for vacations, clothes, shows, and holiday presents—but credit cards were an easy stopgap solution. They qualified for several of these at extremely low introductory rates.

Within two years, one credit card was needed to pay off another and before the end of the third year they were making minimum monthly payments on ten of these plastic debt-anesthetizers. With no end of payments in sight, they refinanced their home and brought down the staggering total of their credit card payments. At this point, Janice was forced to leave her two youngest sons in child-care so she could work full-time. To further save money, the family cut back on vacations, entertainment and clothes as well. It took five more years to recover from the financial trauma, but they eventually pulled out. Since that time, they use just one credit card and pay it off in full each month.

The American Savings Education Council reports that more than half of *parents* roll over credit card debt each month. Four billion invitations for credit cards are sent out each year. That's about one every eight days for each American household. Although most of us throw them away, the companies are rewarded with six hot prospects for every 400 invites. Considering the average U.S. household carries credit card balances of $7500 per year, that equates to an average of $1000 in annual interest paid on these cards alone.

More than a third of us are in the bowl so deep we have little hope of clambering out. An equal number have debt, but pay it on time. Not quite a fourth of us brag about being debt free.

The problem with debt is that people connect its harm only to forfeited money that is doled out to the note-holder; but it's our spirit and soul that are the most compromised. Debt oft-times drives folks to swearing, cheating, escaping, stealing, breaking marriage vows, and even committing suicide.

Interest never sleeps nor sickens nor dies; it never goes to the hospital; it works on Sundays and holidays; it never takes a vacation; it never visits nor travels; it takes no pleasure, it is never laid off work or discharged from employment; it never works on reduced hours…it never pays taxes; it buys no food; it wears no clothes; it is unhoused and without home and so has no repairs, no replacements, no shingling, plumbing, painting, or white-washing; it has neither wife, children, father, mother nor kinfolk to watch over and care for; it has no expense of living; it has neither weddings nor births nor deaths; it has no love, no sympathy; it is as hard and soulless as a granite cliff. *Once in debt, interest is your companion every minute of the day and night; you cannot dismiss it; it yields neither to entreaties, demands, nor orders; and whenever you get in its way or cross its course or fail to meet its demands, it crushes you. –J. Reuben Clark, Jr. "Debt"*

It's a shame that those who are careful with money often get nicknames like penny pincher, miser, and tightwad. (Ironic that the very people who assign these 'tags' are often unwise money users themselves.) Regardless, less than half of us have a budget we stick to.

[SANDRA] *One of my daughters-in-law is from a family of nine children. Right from the beginning, her mother and father decided to use a 70-10-10-10 financial guideline in their household. Even during the years that the*

Dad was a medical student, with education debt highest and income lowest, it is my understanding that they worked hard to live on 70 percent of what they made. The remaining 30 percent was always equally divided between church donations, retirement savings, and their liquid savings account (thus, the 10-10-10 part of the equation). Their pattern of spending and saving continues successfully to this day.

Sure this family believed they could do it, but they also applied the action principle—they **did** it.

Let's look at the money growing on our financial "tree" in yet a different way. We must allow it to grow slowly and patiently with lots of water and fertilizer (consistent small savings) along the way. Winds and maybe even droughts or fire threaten but we recover as quickly as possible and try to keep steadily growing. After the leaves, fruit starts coming. At certain times of the year (or life) we cut back—prune, then watch again as it grows more evenly and lush.

BEWARE WHAT MONEY CAN (AND CAN'T) BUY.

[SANDRA] *A clothing manufacturer in the South reports that his company gets orders for thousands of pairs of men's pants each day. He operates out of a huge warehouse that's easily 3-4 acres under one roof. The owner claims he cannot afford to run his production cost-effectively with two different quality lines, so he makes them all the same high quality. For example, his label-stitchers sew a high-end store label in one run of men's pants, and when orders are complete for that line they sew in a discount department store label. Same style, material, sewing, quality—just another label, and probably an end-price that is many dollars different!*

Money is important but should we spend it on material goods to gain status and confidence? Do we need a brand name to be noticed in life? Do designer clothes offer a great advantage?

[DON] *I was caught in a rainstorm once en route to a media appearance, and rushed into the nearest store to buy a raincoat. It was one of those "pricey" stores, and the cheapest raincoat was $575. The lowest-priced tie was $48— and that was 20 years ago! The salesman proudly said, "People who shop here don't ask prices." Did he really think that I would plunk down some of my hard earned cement pouring, ditch-digging money for a label?*

Nowadays, I refuse to wear a tie with a designer logo on it. I did wear one once— that I received as a gift. I had no idea who Christian Dior, Gucci, Abercrombie or any of those names were that allow ordinary fabric to bear an inflated price tag. A big wheel in New York was setting up a meeting, noticed

Should we spend money to gain status and confidence?

my tie and said, "Well, I know you are somebody because any man who wears Dior is!"

It was the last time I wore that tie.

Anybody with a credit card can wear any brand name.

[DON] *A friend of mine, also a fellow cleaner, lamented that his suitcase was stolen in L.A. as he waited for a cab to unload at the airport. It was a $4500 loss!*

"E-gads! What did you have in that suitcase?" I asked.

"Mostly shirts," he said.

"Shirts! How could you fit $4500 worth of shirts in one suitcase?"

"There were only ten," he said.

One indignant suitcase-less man promptly educated me that $400-600 shirts do exist. He had one on as we spoke. I couldn't see much difference from my own $25 sale special that I'd just bought at the local department store— but I got a lesson in fiber, fabric, and fine stitching despite my protests. Wow! This really was an upscale torso covering. But who would dare sweat in, hug in, or throw a luggage shoulder strap over such a pricey shirt?

Shopping seems to validate some people. We shop for pleasure and satisfaction, not just survival, and we often buy things we can't really afford. Dresses make us look beautiful, lipstick makes us kissable and vitamins make us healthy. We buy things up as fast as advertising is posted in newspaper ads or on the Internet. Successful people don't get caught in this frenzy because they don't feel compelled to *wear* their money.

PUTTING ON THE RITZ.

Often hotels go for the "more is better" strategy in their attempt to appeal to the connoisseur in the most common of us. Isn't a bed and bath about the same everywhere for a tired and dirty body?

[DON] *In the past year alone, I have paid from $35 to $950 for a single night in a hotel. And in all cases the outcome was equivalent. For a bigger buck, it has to be better, we suppose. But how do we improve on such basics as clean sheets and hot water? The last big hotel I stayed in had six pillows on the bed, four bars of soap in various locations, three phones, three mirrors, nine pieces of furniture (besides the bed), and then of course, the towels.*

Admittedly, making the towels a bit thicker and more absorbent is not a bad idea. But this luxury hotel, like so many others, went in for the gargantuan philosophy. I understand that "bath sheet" is the correct term for the towel they supplied. Whatever its name, mine was longer than I was tall, and as awkward to dry with as a king-sized blanket. Their upgraded hand towel was just right for use after my shower. "More" can be a burden.

The successful aren't hooked into this "bigger is better" mentality that results in excesses in, on, and all around us. Yet, if we were asked what would be the best to aid our lives most of us would an- swer... " More Money!"

"If I just had more money, my kids would mind better, my spouse and I would get along, my house would be neater, and I'm sure my dog wouldn't fertilize the lawn anymore. I'd have more friends, more time, more flexibility, and prestige. I could even be more religious."

Some of us think we can buy more of what we want or have more chances to do things our way with money. And that is partly true. Money can free us from some "have-to's." We can pay for our house to be cleaned, our food to be bought and cooked and our dog to be walked if we have enough money. What we sometimes fail to see too late is that many of those down-home "time takers" are the very things that ground us in solid values and purposeful direction. C.S. Lewis said that homemaking is the career for which all others exist; and he may be spot on. Does money work to take us away from our family and home, or to support them?

"If we remember back to the 'hungry years' of our lives, most of us went without luxuries," says Dr. Terry R. Yochum, professional colleague and friend. But most of us probably didn't go without what we truly *needed*. "We reminisce on these difficult, but supremely happy days." In hindsight we often see that the absence of excessive luxuries brings out the best qualities in us. Most successful people have this figured out.

When we really think about it, money isn't too defining. The deserving and the undeserving, the smart or the stupid, can all have it in any amount.

And when we ask certain people who have money as well as those who have little, "What do you plan and dream of doing with your wealth?" often comes one of three quick answers,

"Eat, drink, lounge, play, visit, and travel," *or*

"Do nothing" *or*

"Work to multiply my money."

Money not used to enhance its owner's and others mental, spiritual or physical well-being is of no lasting value. It becomes a taker and a taskmaster that makes decisions for us.

There are also those people who get their money without having to earn it. It doesn't take a genius to see that there is something missing in their lives. *Having is nothing. Earning, doing, and becoming are everything.* Successful people know that accomplishment and sharing is what makes them truly rich.

"MAYBE" MONEY.

Neither of us knows one successful millionaire (and we know many) who spent a penny on the lottery. This isn't because they already have money, but because they believe "choice" not "chance" is the source of fortune in life. Lottery is the simplest of all poor-man's taxation. It is self-inflicted and the few who occasionally win ultimately lose. Studies have shown that lottery winners revert to their previous level of happiness soon after their initial reaction to the great news. There's no glory when they beat the odds, because *they have done nothing to change the conditions that caused them to have nothing.*

The American Gaming Association reports that many people, especially seniors, simply like the socializing end of gambling. With 31 states offering some form of casino gambling (it used to be just Nevada and New Jersey as late as the 1970's), it is now an accepted pastime in our society. Churches and senior centers even offer bus trips to casinos. The biggest problem is that

gambling can sometimes become an addiction. People gamble longer than they plan and often until their last dollar is gone. Using gambling as a way to socialize, or cope with emotional problems or pain is not climbing the ladder out of the toilet, and successful people know it.

The popular book, *The Millionaire Next Door* tells us that 80 percent of millionaires are "first generation affluent"—self-made. They did not amass their wealth from relatives, on game shows, or by gambling or lottery winnings. They are completely down-to-earth types, even hard to identify. Nearly all of them (97 percent) own their own homes and have lived in them for twenty years or more. They are typically married, have three kids, wear inexpensive suits, and drive cars not of the current model year. They are educated and work 45 to 55 hours per week.

This profile surprises most people. I guess we expect millionaires to live a life of luxury and privilege. We assume that because someone has money, they will use it to buy whatever they want. While we don't need to be a millionaire to be successful, we can discover some valuable guidelines from their spending and saving patterns.

Self-made millionaires and others who are successful with their money know there is a big difference between the *ability to pay* for something, and *being able to afford it*. While they might have the power of purchase they use judgment and discretion.

80% of millionaires are "first generation affluent"—self-made.

[SANDRA] *By the time my oldest son finished his ophthalmology residency training two years ago, he was married with two daughters. They were all delighted and relieved to complete the grueling program and finally qualify for the purchase of a modest home following eight years of apartment living. Within a carefully planned budget, they mapped out their student loan repayments, scheduled house payments and allotted money for a necessary second car. They had few discretionary funds left—not enough to furnish their living and family rooms. The couple moved ahead with their frugal plan and avoided the trap of impressing neighbors and relatives by going further into debt with "time" purchases for a new sofa, chairs, appliances or other "accomplishment" trappings. They decided that as his practice grew, so could their accumulations. Necessities would be met, but wants could wait. Guests now file past the carpeted, but empty living room and into their family room where the first piece of furniture, a dining room table with chairs, has finally been purchased—and paid for with cash.*

Financial success is not being fascinated by the accumulation of furnishings, paintings, beating taxes, or even saving to over-buy luxuries. This is almost unrelated to our emotional, spiritual, and physical health—three assets of success that really count. When life's primary focus is on portfolios, it's tempting to lose focus on other purposes of life.

MATURE MONEY.

The goal of retiring with lots of money is about as advantageous as having doctors give you "frequent visit" credit for showing up at their offices. Retiring with something to *do* should be our real future agenda. Time, energy, and love are the things gained in retirement, and money can have only so much impact on those.

Significant worth in life comes from influencing and changing lives for the better, not controlling them with cash. Successful people know counting money is not all that counts.

[SANDRA] *As a service project, my husband and I moved 93-year old Thelma from her apartment to a private care facility. She had fallen and required assisted living care. The new home would also be much closer to our own so that our children could visit with her occasionally, as she had no family of her own.*

Although Thelma realizes her remaining earth years are few, she is consumed with saving her money, and has been since she began work more than 75 years ago. All of her concerns and thoughts point toward preserving and making more money.

"What kind of work did you do all your life, Thelma?" I asked.

"I was a civil service worker. First a clerk stenographer, then I worked in personnel over in Los Angeles."

"What else did you do?"

"Nothing really. I was married three times and divorced, but no children. I was a careful saver. Maybe a little too frugal," she admits. "I watched the paper for coupons and sales and drove on weekends anywhere to get the best prices. And if it wasn't too far, I would even walk to save some gas. I hardly ever bought clothes, but when I did, they had to be on a really good sale. And I used them for years until they were worn out—completely. I never replaced my furniture that I can remember. All of the money in my savings is from going without."

"Have you ever done any traveling?" I asked.

"I drove to a few places a long time ago, but I've never really been to any big cities outside of L.A. and for sure not out of the country. It costs too much to travel and see things, so I've really never been anywhere."

"Would you like to go on a trip with our family sometime?"

"I'm too old to go anyplace now. And I still don't feel good about wasting money to go on a trip."

My husband and I returned to Thelma's apartment to sort and gather her clothing and personal affects. In her closet hung an eclectic array of 50-year-old clothes, some with sale-priced tags still dangling. Chipped dishes and cracked china filled cupboards that were themselves chipped and cracked. Her stove was small and so old the door had sprung to a permanently jarred-open position. Every piece of furniture was split and worn through to the foam padding. The whole apartment looked like a bulldozer had pushed old junk into a discarded stockpile.

On our subsequent visits with Thelma, she complained about her unmanageable long, white hair, but refused to allow her money to be spent on a cut and perm which the in-house beautician could provide. She would

Significant worth in life comes from influencing and changing lives for the better, not controlling them with cash. Successful people know counting money is not all that counts.

consider a cheap home permanent "if you can find one on a good sale," she informed me.

In Thelma's outdated purse with its broken handle, she had me search for a pair of tweezers one day. I found them, but they were too corroded to use. Other purse objects included broken eyeglasses, melted lipstick and even used Q-tips.

Ironically, in Thelma's bank account that she asked my husband to help her with, he discovered nearly two million dollars. The money had sat idle as far as its benefit to Thelma, except for the interest it earned. This amassing of wealth took place over a lifetime at minimum wage salary. At her passing, the entire estate went to a university she had never even attended.

Thelma had a mindset to save, not live. She was as much a slave to her abundance of wealth as some of us who are yoked to our accumulation of debt. Lots of money doesn't necessarily mean lots of success.

The value of money is to free us up for service and love. It is to keep the mind and body tuned into, and caring for those in real need. What good is a large *net worth* without a *personal net* filled with people, places, and purposes that add sparkle, meaning and dignity to our lives?

SUCCESSFUL PEOPLE SPEND MONEY WELL.

We asked the question to young and old, "What is the best thing you have ever bought with your money—any amount (large or small) that brought you the most satisfaction/reward for the amount you spent?"

- *"I saved up my allowance for three years beginning when I was about 9 years old. Eventually I had enough to buy what I always wanted: a puppy. For most kids, a puppy was a minor distraction from their everyday misery, and once the puppy becomes a dog it wasn't even worth that anymore. Not for me. I loved my dog with all my heart. My dog became my best friend and went with me everywhere, "Milo", a Brittany that cost $250, eased me into young adulthood by helping me gain confidence and allowing me to have companionship. As I grew up, however, I began needing Milo less and less, and we eventually stopped our normal activities of dog training and attending dog shows. My mom (who is a die-hard dog lover) took up where I left off and I have never seen her happier. My mom used to show dogs but it became too difficult for her to work full time, raise us kids, and continue her hobby. Now she had again reached a point in her life* where she needed Milo and I'm glad he was there to give back to her. Milo was definitely the best thing I ever bought with my money."—Danielle

•"I like to buy stationery. Even though it is somewhat expensive, I enjoy decorating my letters with stickers and I really feel like I'm making my pen pals happy. Maybe my letter will brighten their day a little bit. I write letters to brothers and sisters away at college and on missions, to friends on vacation and that have moved away, and even to old boyfriends."
—Natalee

•"I bought weight-lifting equipment. Not only do I use it, but I also share it with my friends. They come over and we work out together. I got the best use for my money, because my weights are key to helping me feel stronger, healthier and more confident."—Rick

•"In June of 2000, I flew to Cordoba, Argentina, for a chiropractic seminar. After the event, I traveled by plane and then drove six hours by car to see a friend who was dying from colon cancer. I spent an entire week with him and his family. After I left, his doctor was to perform surgery, but he died six months later. I thank God for allowing me to have the means and giving me the opportunity to see my dear friend one more time in a very small, remote

town. It was very hard to get there, but my money was well spent."
—Raul

•"I have enough financial reserve so I don't have to scramble when the cows get out, or the dogs eat all the chickens so-to-speak. I guess some people call this mad money or contingency planning. Whatever its name… it works well!"—John

•"The best thing we can do with our money is have children. They are the source of all happiness and legacy in the total scheme of things. Sure, it's taxing some times, but in the final analysis, we cannot find anything more satisfying in our life than progeny. They cost, but they are more than worth the investment!"—Joyce

•"To have a decent camera and take and distribute pictures frequently, will be the best use of any dollars I might have kicking around. Photos are a gift that is inexpensive, but one of a kind. A photo lives forever on a page and in a mind and conveys messages that someone cares enough to capture the very best. It doesn't really cost a lot either."—Dennis

•"Lessons and more lessons. I spend a few dollars on piano, mechanic, safety, swimming, and other lessons. They return over 1000% emotional, spiritual and often even financial gains. *Buy them for yourself or for others, even strangers. Their eventual talent becomes in part your doing. Nothing can make you feel better."—Dean*

• *"The best money I spent this year (and I spent thousands on dingy things) was when I bought a nice Roget's Thesaurus."—A Poet*

• *"The best money I ever spent was when Barbara and I were the poorest. We were going to school, raising young kids, trying to run a business and make payroll. We didn't have a spare dime. I worked at night, cleaning, and earned an extra $400 that Barbara knew nothing about. On Christmas day, she unwrapped the usual $3 household gifts we all give a mom. Then she opened the envelope with the ticket to Alaska to see her mother whom she hadn't seen for three years. She cried and I told her to go for two weeks and I would handle things at home. She didn't even pack and was out of there like a shot. The trip proved to be one of the best things ever for her and her mother and for me!"—Don*

Money is a positive force when it is spent to enhance the quality of life of its owners and others.

Just because I live simply, with little, doesn't mean I don't understand mystery and complexity. That is why I live simply. -Anon.

THE SIMPLE LIFE REQUIRES LESS MONEY.

There is more to poverty than lack of money, just as there is more to fulfillment than financial increase. Many of the deepest joys in life are not dependent on having or spending lots of money.

[SANDRA] *With six Eagle Scout sons, I know a bit about the scouting program. Without a doubt, my boys' favorite merit badge was camping. I used to think males naturally had this strong desire to connect with dirt, hard ground, bugs, blisters and other mementos of adventure. Not until later did I learn that they simply preferred the freedom to experience some joys of uncomplicated living. No bed sheets, blankets and spread to fiddle with— just a bedroll to stuff in a bag. No dishwasher to load, floor to mop or table to set—just a fish to catch and fry in a pan. No pictures on walls to dust—just pictures of nature to photograph.*

In reality, my boys got a break from the demands of every day living with its accumulations—all of which suited them just fine. It's refreshing to leave collections of the world, and experience things of the earth again.

Spending the night under the stars beats spending money on movie stars.

The media, by featuring its "stars," shows off so much celebrity opulence that we don't believe we have enough ourselves. We equate satisfaction with stardom. We see, of course, only the polished side of their lives. Anytime we make judgments and comparisons and establish our values on distorted evidence, we've got toilet trouble. Anyone who watches the masses spend their money believes that everyone has more than they do. It's simply a *mob money mentality.*

ROOT OF EVIL?

Money is the root of much frustration. Most of us are obsessed with making it, spending it, borrowing it, saving it or are frustrated from *not* having it. This money fixation we are all too familiar with, is the basis of most meetings, arguments, divorces, and even murder cases. Ninety-nine percent of us believe "If I had more, I'd be more."

> *"Too many of us equate our self-worth with our net worth."*
> —Nancy Everson

Balancing receivables and payables never seems to end

If we retraced our most trying times in life, for many of us money would be front and center.

[DON] *I've never felt that money was my measure of success, yet the most miserable parts of building my business were money concerns. The work hours, competition, travel, and conditions of the business were pure enjoyment but collecting and scrambling to get money for payroll after payroll for more than* ten years, was pure misery. Balancing receivables and payables with bank loan commitments seemed to never end. I've also watched hundreds of my employees focus on paychecks, always frustrated and needing more. Certainly in these days "enough" is easy to earn. All of us believe when and if we become successful, money will never be an issue again. Forget that dream! Money—its bleeding and needing, will never go away. The only recourse to stop it from putting our lives in the toilet is to control it—own it without it owning us.

RARE ADVICE ON MONEY FROM 25 SUCCESSFUL PEOPLE

- Don't GAMBLE: There's no enjoyment in losing money. What you win you deem free and generally waste it anyway.
- Leave the LOTTERY alone. Period.
- I used to BORROW Money carelessly. It was so easy to get but a dilemma to figure out how to pay back.
- Have you ever added up all of your EATING OUT costs? Americans spend more money each week at restaurants than at the grocery store. We try to cut back to one meal "out" each week.
- The OWNERSHIP of motor homes and boats wasn't worth the ten years paying for them.
- I gave MY KIDS too much and for too long. I've learned that adult kids need to be on their own.

- I Love those HOBBIES like horses, golf and flying but I learned to make them a remote supplement, not a priority, to my happy living.
- "Two hundred pairs of SHOES, do you think that's too many?" my neighbor asked me once. I get along fine on four pair.
- The over elaborate wedding PARTY. What a mistake! We make all our parties and weddings nice but not exorbitant.
- When we got that INSURANCE money we just blew it. Now we carefully invest any unexpected windfalls.
- I've grown to hate the words "A GOOD DEAL" from investors.
- COLLECTIONS have no stopping place—and no storing place. I had too many—so I cut them down to one group.
- A luxury VACATION? We never spend what we can't pay back in one month.
- In my last HUNTING trip I figured that what I caught cost me about $117 a pound. My wife buys better meat a block away at $2.17 a pound, so I gave up the habit.
- It took me three years to realize my judgment on extravagant CAR purchases was clearly ego, not for transportation; I gave up impractical extras and saved a bundle.
- We were living in twice the HOUSE we needed—and paying twice the cost. After moving to a more appropriate-sized home, we had

enough money left to double our retirement contribution.

- The big DIAMOND I bought was really for me, not her—when people saw it on her hand they would say: "Lucille, you must have a great husband." Ego is brainless. After awhile we realized there's also some risk to her safety when she sports a rock like that. So, she gave it up for a solid band. It was a bright move.
- I only used one third of all my electric TOOLS, so I gave away some and sold others. I gained friends, space and pocket change all in one brilliant decision.
- Unless it's a rare exception, SOUVENIRS are 98% a waste of space and money. And these days, whom do they impress? I never buy or bring them home any more.
- MOVIES, concerts and ball games are so expensive, I selectively choose just a few to enrich my life—and I don't feel deprived. I used to spend all my extra money attending some function every single weekend. Now I can let it go and I'm better for it.
- I found out that we spend more for hair restoration, VANITY products, and glamour than for all the dental costs in the entire U.S.! Soon after learning that I gave up coloring my completely gray hair and wearing fake fingernails. People love me more for it.
- I quit HANGING OUT with spenders and those who shopped around just for something to do.

- When I carry lots of CASH I spend it fast. With little cash on me, I can go weeks with the same life quality.
- Paying lots for an EDUCATION doesn't mean you're educated. Instead of automatically feeling we need to send our kids to the most expensive undergraduate institutions, we work with them to find good, less pricey schools and to qualify for scholarships. A good education is more about the effort of the child than the number of endowed chairs at the school.

Eventually only one expert on money counts—YOU. Money is an individual thing: *how* we get it, *how much* we get and *what we do* with it. Certainly these days there are plenty of options and opinions! So why all the concern and confusion over it? One hundred years ago, Robert Service just plain nailed it with his beginning verses of the "Spell of the Yukon".

SPELL OF THE YUKON
I wanted the gold, and I sought it;
I scrabbled and mucked
like a slave.
Was it famine or scurvy
I fought it?
I hurled my youth into a grave.
I wanted the gold, and I got it
Came out with a fortune
last fall
Yet somehow life's not what
I thought it,
And somehow the gold isn't all.

In the scramble for wealth or the rat race for riches, if not careful, we may change slowly from a man or a woman into a machine. It happens so subtly we may not even feel the gears taking over.

Money may come easily or with difficulty, but have you ever stopped to think how quickly it can all be taken away? Death, sickness, economic downturn, lawsuits, divorce, or war can all deplete resources in a flash. Think of *losing* it all when you are *giving your all* to get it.

MONEY-WISE.

Parents fuss and worry about it, but we still manage to tell our kids the basics about the birds and the bees. But for money instruction, most kids grow up without a clue. Then they slip into adulthood still paying meager attention to this critical part of their lives. The old adage, "A fool and his money are soon parted" needs a new paradigm—"A man can be made a fool by the use of his money."

The big problem with our view of money is not so much our having it, or getting and spending it—it's the concern that someone else has *more* than we do. In other words, it's not that we don't have enough, it's that others have more.

In the new century, the scramble for more money has intensified into some archetype demanding a net worth—the supposed ultimate measurement of man's accomplishment. Money somehow defines the security of an individual—when the real worth of people is

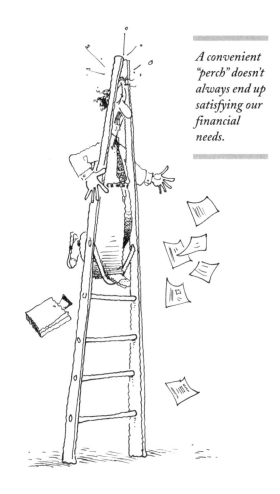

A convenient "perch" doesn't always end up satisfying our financial needs.

their good influence, not their stocks and bonds. Financial investment can return only money. Influence can return money as well as happiness for others and us.

An executive of a major U.S. company told us this story,

When I first hired people they had tears of thankfulness just to have a good job. I paid them well and they thanked me and were happy, secure, and stable. Then one year I did something I had not done before—I shared profits in the form of a bonus. So at end of the year, knowing it would make them happy, weld them in and improve productivity, I handed them out. After that, the evolution of our bonus giving went something like,

- *First year, 'I'm happy to have a job with good pay.'*
- *Second year, 'Thank you for the bonus.'*
- *Third year, 'I deserve the bonus.'*
- *Fourth year, 'How come my bonus isn't bigger?'*

By the sixth year, almost all of the employees were worrying about, finagling, chiseling and projecting what their bonuses would be, not appreciating their jobs or the significant base salaries they were getting. I have watched many of my employees and their families getting poorer in life as they were getting richer in money.

More money allowed more luxury and convenience, but not necessarily more satisfaction. In an Aesop-like fable, we learn of a successful rancher who had eight neighbors surrounding him with smaller ranches who were struggling to make a living, but managing okay. The rancher, who owned the most property, needed to annex a few of these adjacent parcels of land for a more efficient operation. He offered a very generous $1 million dollars to each of his eight neighbors to buy their smaller places. All decided to hold out for

more—so, the large rancher, being wise in money matters, took another approach.

He anonymously mailed $500,000 dollars to each neighbor. Because they were always short of money, at first there was much rejoicing. The neighbors began to improve their standard of living and they bought things they always wanted but could never afford: newer cars, bigger houses, recreation vehicles and pools. These things raised their insurance rates, spoiled their kids, and heightened their expectations for additional wants. Within three years all of them had overspent their money, bloated themselves with new toys and social circles that put them in a bracket of expense their former income couldn't afford. In other words, they didn't have the earning power to support their current spending level but couldn't turn back. Each of them went bankrupt and eventually had to sell. The large farmer now offered $500,000 for their remaining assets, which they were grateful to walk away with. He acquired all of the land for his original priced offer.

[DON] *The love of money or of a bargain can poison our thinking. Down the road a block from our offices in Pocatello, Idaho, a group of nine skinny, little ballerinas were holding a car wash to earn money for a dance event they wanted to compete in. On the hottest day of the year they were sweating and working their little hearts out (they couldn't even reach the top of my car)—willing to work for a trip instead of begging for money. It was a donation wash, meaning they washed the car and you paid what you felt was fair.*

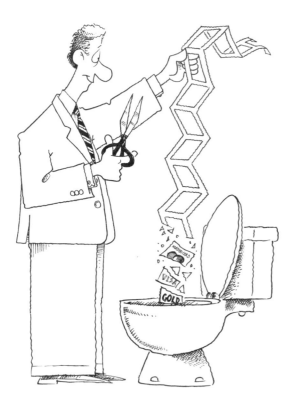

The spirit of most of those in line before me was to get the best for the least money. People in $70,000 Land Rovers with rhino bars, were eeking out maybe $2, $3, or $5 dollars for these girls and bragging what a deal they got. They could have used their money to lift and enlighten and bless, but loved the dollars more than the cause of nine little sunburned girls.

Money can and will do ugly, unsuccessful things to us if we let it. *Having* can make us *less* giving and sharing, not necessarily more generous. But the rich and poor alike can be prideful in what they have or seek. One thing holds true, when we worry more about our assets than people, we won't be successful. Money is a tool and it's here to stay. It can make us merry or miserable, all depending on how we use it. It can put us in the toilet or on top of the world.

Successful people spend less than they make, and they share their assets with more than themselves. It's just that simple.

We have three basic choices when it comes to handling our money. We can,
1. *Spend less than we make*
2. *Spend all that we make*
3. *Spend more than we make*

Most successful people are not working for the money. They're working for the rewards…the satisfaction…the challenge of it.

Rewards

As we observe the walls and halls of our homes and offices, we do not have to wonder what America's real pastime is. Forget baseball and apple pie! Our "turn on" is to get rewards. We dust off more plaudit-worded wall plaques, oversized trophies, cups, pen sets, medals, ribbons, autographed books, and cruise certificates than we do furniture.

We collect pats on the back like starving junkyard dogs. We'll buy 80% faster when we are offered a "free" reward with purchase. We live for rewards in one form or the other and love to be decorated and recognized for any gain of any size. Truly we've become "benefit bounty hunters." Like trained dolphins, we'll "jump through any hoop" to get a fish. We have to have a *dessert* in life for any identifiable deed. We look forward to the sales award, trophy, the trip, and the applause, the announcement or name in the newspaper.

Far past the gadgetry of souvenirs, or even commissions or bonuses, we want big rewards in the end. If we attend something, we expect an attendance award; if we return a lost item, there has to be recognition. We play the lottery for a minuscule chance of a reward. We form the bowling team not just to bowl, but also to get the big trophy for showing up. We generously donate to worthy causes, whose people turn around and spend a big chunk of the money on engraved thank you plaques. Attaining champion status isn't enough reward; we *need* tangible, complimentary praise and the publicity to go with it.

Think of what sells magazines. There are promises of a reward—in diet, decoration, bodybuilding, sex relationships and travel, to name a few.

The real question is: what are **worthy** rewards? Why break our behinds for a measly free ball cap, paper certificate, or attendance award? Kids and adults alike often ask parents and employers the

same big question, "If I do these duties what do I get? "I ate my broccoli, visited the sick neighbor, drove safe for ten years, got my degree and planted a garden. Now what?"

As virtue is its own reward, so should good health, ordinary solvency, friends, education, and freedom be their own reward. The value of controlling time, money, relationships, being law abiding and practicing good health, yields indescribable, ever-lasting satisfaction— hence rewards.

The prizes given out on popular game shows have always baffled us. The *Price is Right* sets money values on furniture, cars, boats, stereos, and appliances. People salivate as each of the prizes go on display. If the show host gave less tangible items instead, like violin lessons, a service expedition, two months at a youth camp, a scholarship, a personal visit with a professional organizer, or a small business to run, you wouldn't hear a peep from the baffled onlookers. It is more common to respond to the "visible" rewards than the intrinsic ones, which seldom get eulogized.

THE REWARDS OF SETTLING FOR THE *UP* IN UPGRADE.

Our businesses require lots of travel out of Salt Lake and Los Angeles. We've logged more than four million air miles between us, which has given us an opportunity to observe plenty of people trying to get a seat upgrade—meaning flying first class instead of coach. These priority seats are a little bigger, food comes with its own tablecloth, and headphones and drinks are complimentary.

[DON] *I watch folks demean themselves as they crowd, beg, cry, threaten, and demand that the airline gate agent give them first class service. My lifetime accumulation of award miles usually puts me ahead on the list of most upgrade-seekers. Often I have the agent come back to me in "coach" and say, "Mr. Aslett, we have an upgrade in first class for you." Generally, if I already have empty seats next to me, I don't consider the upgrade an advantage, and refuse. Everyone around, including the agent, is shocked. Who could refuse the reward of an upgrade?*

Is more luxury necessarily an upgrade? Not always. Lasting life quality can come in privacy more often than with someone waiting on us in overplush conditions. Having privacy and space back in the coach section of a plane or in a non-crowded, quiet, but tiny hotel room, beats the big and the best in the overkill of luxury.

Better relates much more to freedom than to luxury. Upscale isn't always an upgrade in life. With rewards we are tempted to head to pretty, before precious, and seek quantity over quality.

Here are nine genuine, lasting rewards that will come to all of us as we successfully live our lives out of the toilet.

9. You'll get out of the recovery room.

8. You will keep better company.

7. You will spend less money and get more.

6. You'll find extra time.

5. People will treat you better!

4. Your creativity will be revealed.

3. You will be energized.

2. You'll look better.

1. You'll feel better physically, mentally and spiritually.

1. You'll feel better physically, mentally and spiritually. Feeling better motivates almost everything. What finer reward is worth going after than this? To feel good all the time!

2. You'll look better. Once, Abraham Lincoln didn't hire a man he was interviewing for a political post. When asked by his Secretary of State, "Why?" he said, "I didn't like his face." Shocked by his answer, the Secretary said, "Mr. Lincoln, he can't help how he looks!" Lincoln replied, "After a man is eight years old, he is responsible for what his face looks like." In other words, success shows in your countenance—your face, eyes, walk, and overall bearing—and portrays how confident you feel. Cosmetics come off in the heat of the battle, but genuine character stays stable 24 hours a day. Active is attractive when people are doing the right things for the right reasons. It's common these days to be decorated with accolades, but keeping far out of the toilet in regular living gives you that commodity called class.

3. You will be energized. Successful people arise early, happy and invigorated in the morning. To get the most out of every day is their goal. One reason you'll have more energy and motivation is because you haven't spent it on trivial struggle time. You won't get tired even when others think you should be tired. Success gives you stamina, while struggling saps it. We might parallel this concept of our lives to ships whose hull is underwater. Without being noticed, barnacles begin to build and gradually cause a "drag" affect. The boat won't slide through the water as efficiently as before. The more the build-up and accumulation of barnacles, the more the drag. The boat needs more and more fuel just to be propelled. As the accumulation of unnecessary baggage causes you to go slower, spent energy on the unimportant makes you feel sluggish.

Stop, clean and polish the hull and the boat leaps ahead freely with renewed acceleration. It always feels so good to run without dragging excess. When life's barnacles exit it gives us the freedom and reserve power to run efficiently and unbeatably! We automatically have more energy.

4. Your creativity will be revealed. Creative people get lots of comments and praise. You can be one of them! Creativity is rich in *all* minds, but generally so buried in piles of "stuff" we are plodding through, we cannot find it, let alone use it! Success un-smothers a spiritual depth everyone has in rich abundance. When our time is spent coping with frequent dips in the toilet, we have less time; hence little experience with our creative talent. *Just think of all the dreams and ideas that just die somewhere in us.* Creativity is there and asks only to be activated. Successful living allows this creativity to surface by simply unfettering our future.

5. People will treat you better! As much as people (friends, family, boss, peers) might pity us for any unfortunate condition we may be in, they won't treat us entirely well—in fact they often cleverly avoid us, secretly wishing we would go away. Others have enough of their own burdens without adding on any of ours. We patronize or ignore those with continual woes and toilet overflows.

Being treated better is one prime reason to make up your mind to stay out of the toilet.

A consultant was called to a school district where morale among the custodians wasn't just in the toilet; it was down the sewer. The maintenance personnel were sour, critical, defensive and lazy, to the point that the school administration could do nothing. The kids hated the janitors, and the janitors hated the kids. The buildings were so dirty you could practically get an airborne disease just inhaling. Life was awful for everyone, and nothing seemed likely to change.

The speaker's job was to motivate this motley crew to function some degree above the present. He gave 150 of them an enthusiastic explanation of why and how to get life out of the hundreds of toilets they cleaned. He shared his experiences of overcoming bad attitude and of doing some positive public relations in even the worst circumstances. And he did it with humor. They all listened, laughed, and left; but one janitor out of all of them caught the

vision and truly internalized the message. He started wearing a uniform, cleaned his custodial closets, organized his equipment, talked to the students, came in early, followed up on requests and cheerfully volunteered for extra duties. Instantly the whole school swung to his aid, helped him clean, loved him, and praised him—even brought him cookies. His part of the school building was now spotless—and his life, through a job he began to love—was turned around. People treated him to the level to which he raised himself. The rest of the janitors, content to stay where they were, rode their pitiful conditions to retirement, accepting the disdain of others.

6. You'll find extra time.

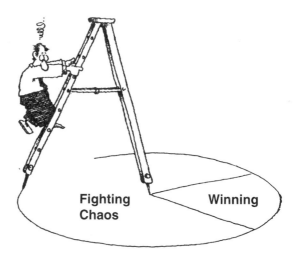

Most people use the precious hours allotted to us on earth in just this proportion. Constant chaos is not necessary *unless* we allow ourselves to live in the toilet zone. Once we get out, we can reverse that sign to:

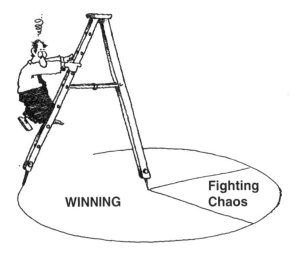

WINNING

Fighting Chaos

If there are two major issues most all people are struggling with in trying to attain a happy life, it is battling the *too busy* and *the too much*. The reason most of us are too busy is simply because we *own* too much. Our problems are cut in half, when excess exits from our life. Most chaos and trivia is in the toilet. If we are in there with it, it is or will become part of us. Success separates us from the sacks of baggage we carry labeled "trouble." When the "too much" is gone, more room is left in our hearts, minds and homes.

7. You will spend less money and get more. Now this is a deal! Successful people *have* their own bargain and don't have to go hunting (shopping) for some illusive solution to their self-esteem. A big slice of the quality of our life is determined by how much peace we can get from the money we spend.

8. You will keep better company. We can love all of mankind but don't have to live with them. Success is a strong automatic friend selector freeing us to choose the best companions. Walking with the wise (out of the toilet) will go a long way to making us wise.

9. You'll get out of the recovery room. As a national past time we buy into recovery with the philosophy of, first, foul life up, now fix it. Almost every news and story line plot (especially in the movies) is about getting into trouble, then finding a clever way to get out. Getting sick, or injured, or caught, is okay because we can rally other resources to save us. Bad idea! The real reward is our ability to avoid the bowl. Movie cowboys are the only ones who recover from wounds in a week! Sympathy cards and therapy sessions are not as sound as avoidance. *Successful* means not making reservations for the recovery room.

The best rewards are sometimes disguised. It's not always what you *get* but what you *become* when all areas of your life are out of the toilet. You will feel order and energy coming your way.

We need to be able to look forward to something sunny, renewing and promising—right now! The ultimate prize here is that these rewards for successfully keeping life out of the toilet can be yours. **Climb out! Today!**

MORE ... FROM DON ASLETT AND SANDRA PHILLIPS

GRANDMA'S Quick Fixes — SANDRA PHILLIPS

Handy help for the next planned or surprise visits from your little ones. — Fun.

How Successful People... Keep Their Lives Out Of The Toilet — Five Fundamental Principles — SANDRA PHILLIPS • DON ASLETT

You've read it, now share it with friends, employees, and others. Volume discounts up to 50% off.

HOW TO HAVE A 48-HOUR DAY — GET TWICE AS MUCH DONE AS YOU DO NOW! — DON ASLETT

You can beat the clock and calendar! Double your daily effectiveness.

Speaking
- Team and individual keynote and lecture programs offered on all book topics to corporations-clubs-educational institutions-church groups-businesses-homeshows

Products
- Innovations to make home care quick and fun
- *The Cleanest Home in America* design project
- CD's, videos on low-maintenance living

Consulting
- Review domestic and commercial plans for maintenance-free building concepts
- Book writing seminars

To Order:
www. InHomeVations.com
InHomeVations
1578 Cloister Drive
La Habra Heights, CA 90631

InHomeVations

email:
Sandra@InHomeVations.com